The Mass Production of Memory

MEM

A Volume in the Series
Public History in Historical Perspective
Edited by
Marla R. Miller

THE MASS PRODUCTION OF

1ORY

Travel and Personal Archiving in the Age of the Kodak

TAMMY S. GORDON

University of Massachusetts Press

Amherst and Boston

Copyright © 2020 by University of Massachusetts Press
All rights reserved
Printed in the United States of America
ISBN 978-1-62534-532-5 (paper); 531-8 (hardcover)
Designed by Kristina Kachele Design, llc
Set in TheSerif with Isodora Sans Alt and NewYorkerPlus Light display
Indexing by Amron Gravett, Wild Clover Book Services
Printed and bound by Books International, Inc.
Cover design by Kristina Kachele Design, llc
Cover photo: Detail of page from an album belonging to Cadaine Hairston
documenting a trip to Keansburg Beach in New Jersey in 1924. Robert Langmuir
African American Photograph Collection, Stuart A. Rose Manuscript, Archives,
and Rare Book Library, Emory University.

Library of Congress Cataloging-in-Publication Data
Names: Gordon, Tammy S., 1967– author.
Title: The mass production of memory : travel and personal archiving in the age
of the Kodak / Tammy S. Gordon.
Description: Amherst : University of Massachusetts Press, [2020] | Series: Public
history in historical perspective | Includes bibliographical references and index. |
Identifiers: LCCN 2020019222 | ISBN 9781625345318 (hardcover) |
ISBN 9781625345325 (paperback) | ISBN 9781613767825 (ebook) |
ISBN 9781613767818 (ebook)
Subjects: LCSH: Travel photography—United States—History—20th century. |
Vernacular photography—United States—History—20th century. | Eastman
Kodak Company—History—20th century. | Tourism—United States—History—
20th century. | Photography—Social aspects—United States—History—20th
century.
Classification: LCC TR790 .G67 2020 | DDC 771—dc23
LC record available at https://lccn.loc.gov/2020019222

British Library Cataloguing-in-Publication Data
A catalog record for this book is available from the British Library.

To a new generation of camera users addressing the inequities enacted in and through public spaces.

The . . . big idea behind the selling of Eastman Kodaks is that every man can write the outline of his own history, and that the outline will be a hundredfold more interesting if it is illustrated.
—C. B. Larrabee, writing in the advertising trade magazine *Printer's Ink,* 1922

Everyman his own historian.
—Carl L. Becker, Presidential Address to the American Historical Association, 1931

CONTENTS

Acknowledgments *xi*

Introduction
   "The story is complete for all time"
   Mass Photography for the Future of History *1*

Chapter One
   "One did not 'take' a camera"
   The Roots of Tourist Photography *15*

Chapter Two
   "The World is mine—I own a KODAK"
   Marketing Memory and Privilege *25*

Chapter Three
   "Side Trips in Camera-Land"
   Tourism and the Visual Record *39*

Chapter Four
"When I Send You a Picture of Berlin"
The Memory Emergency of the First World War *71*

Chapter Five
"A visible token"
Expanding the Promise of the Kodak in the Interwar Years *91*

Conclusion
The Legacy of the First Generation of Mass Tourism
and Portable Photography *117*

Notes *131*

Index *153*

ACKNOWLEDGMENTS

If it were not for the support of the excellent people (and a couple of non-humans) around me and the desire to know answers to my own questions, this book would have died a thousand times. I desperately hope I have not forgotten anyone here in the thank-yous. Please forgive me if I have.

I am especially lucky to have worked with supportive colleagues who shaped this book with their questions, comments, travel experiences, and general goodwill and good cheer. The folks in the History Department at NC State University are truly great people. I would like to thank Courtney Hamilton, who helped me through all the budget issues and travel strategies required for research. She facilitates travel for all of us, keeping us moving and thinking. Likewise Ingrid Hoffius finds ways to support graduate students' travel, making their educations richer and my workload a bit lighter. Fellow public historians Matthew Booker, Kat Charron, Frederico Freitas, Craig Friend, Blair Kelley, Susanna Lee, Alicia McGill, and David Zonderman provide models for engaged scholarship that make me proud to work with them. Our conversations about public history keep my brain zipping. I am likewise inspired by David

Ambaras, Ross Bassett, Dean Bruno, Megan Cherry, Ebony Jones, and Julia Rudolph. Special thanks to David A. and Kat for reading and commenting on parts of this book when it was at its most drafty. I am so grateful to colleagues at UNC Wilmington for supporting this work, granting a semester's sabbatical to dive into the scholarship on tourism, and commenting on the ideas in development at Faculty Friday. I am grateful for conversations with Ken Shefsiek and Paul Townend. Thank you to Will Moore and the Boston University American and New England Studies Program for the opportunity to be a part of your lively intellectual community. Lisa Pollard, Lynn Mollenauer, Candice Bredbenner, and Sue McCaffray: thank you for sharing your smarts, your humor, your wine, and the occasional weekend of conversations about life, history, and border crossing.

The graduate students in the Public History Program at North Carolina State University are exceptionally smart and highly motivated to apply historical thinking and knowledge to contemporary problem solving. Being a part of your education is an honor, and your quick wits and intellectual creativity have made this book and my work in general more useful. I am particularly grateful for conversations with doctoral scholars Kawan Allen, Petros Apostolopolous, Raiza Baez Calderon, Matthew Champagne, Amanda Finn, Marilyn Drath, Alex Goodrich, Shima Hosseininasab, Chris Laws, JoCora Moore, Many Paige-Lovingood, Katie Schinabeck, Sarah Soleim, Holly Smith, Gevorg Vardanyan, Troy Burton, and fellow travelers Lisa Withers and Melody Hunter-Pillion. The future of our field is very exciting because you are a part of it.

Transnational exchange made this book much better. The opportunities to attend the International Federation for Public History conferences in Bogotá, Colombia, and Ravenna, Italy, facilitated important conversations that made me think more deeply about what it means to be a visitor. At these meetings, I especially appreciated the collegiality of Alix Green, David Dean, Beatriz Sanchez Bagnarello, Joan Zenzen, Serge Noiret, Thomas Cauvin, and Michael Frisch. Thank you to the University of Hertfordshire Department of History for including me in History Weekend and asking excellent questions about Kodak. Colleagues Jaroslav Ira and Linda Kovarova of Charles University in Prague are working at the interface of heritage and history, and their work is a true inspiration. Thank you for including me in conversations at the EU seminar on heritage and resilience and for inviting me to work as a TEMA+ scholar. I look forward to our future collaborations. I owe a great deal to the late

Lud'a Klusáková, who provided a model of transnational collaboration in public history and who asked exceptionally helpful questions about this project. You were a true scholar and mentor, and I miss you.

Archivists are awesome. At the George Eastman Museum, I owe a debt of gratitude for the help of Joseph Struble, Photography Collection archivist (now retired), and Jesse Peers, George Eastman Legacy Collection archivist. My summer visits to Rochester were much more productive and enjoyable because of your work. Thank you. Maxine Friedman of Staten Island Historical Society was essential to the study of Alice Austen's work and life. William A. Peniston of the Newark Museum Archives was a skilled guide through the Broner Collection and helped me to locate other sources around Newark. I am also grateful to everyone at the Rubenstein Library at Duke University and the Southern Historical Collection at the Wilson Library at UNC Chapel Hill. Thank you so much to all the archivists and collections managers whose work has resulted in digital access. I am particularly grateful to the Hartman Center for Sales, Marketing, and Advertising History at Duke University, the Beineke Library at Yale University, the Schlesinger Library of Harvard University, Princeton University's Department of Art and Archaeology, the Kautz Family YMCA Archives at the University of Minnesota Library, and collector Trent Kelley for their excellent online collections. Earnestine Keaton's work with the Lower Bladen Columbus Historical Society and family archiving is an inspiration for preserving and sharing family and community history. People with legacy photography skills, like Emanuel and Ernest Cole of the Fotoshoppe in Cary, North Carolina, help produce new images from the old ways, and I am grateful for their skills with developing photos from my Kodak Brownie. The D. H. Hill Jr. Library at North Carolina State University runs on the work of some of the most brilliant, reflective, engaged information science folks I have ever been privileged to work with. The Ask Us Desk, Digital Media Services, Special Collections and Archives, Outreach and Engagement: you all rock! I particularly enjoy working with Virginia Ferris and Todd Kosmerick. Thank you all for your skills, commitment, and professionalism.

Colleagues I've met through international education initiatives contributed new insights on making meaning when traveling. Thank you to the North Carolina State University Global Fellows in Prague, especially Debbie Acker, senior associate director for operations and academic programs for the Shelton Leadership Center, for working on study abroad for first-generation and economically disadvantaged college students and Madhusudan Katti, associate professor, Forestry and Environmental Resources, for insight on the connections between public science and public history and for giving me some experience in how an ornithologist photographs a city. Both Sean Addley and Megan Winzeler of the NC State European Center are brilliant in facilitating international education, and I am lucky to work with them. Specialists in many different areas related to intercultural skills meet yearly at the Workshop in Intercultural Skills Enhancement organized by Wake Forest University, and it is here that I gain interdisciplinary insights on border crossing and education.

I am much obliged to everyone at University of Massachusetts Press, particularly Marla Miller and Matt Becker. Thank you to the anonymous reviewers of the manuscript for their careful readings and productive critique. Rachael DeShano and Amanda Heller made this book much better with their attention to the details.

Thank you to all of my friends for kindness and support during the time I worked on this book. I am especially grateful for my fellow aikidoka at Hemlock Bluffs Aikido for keeping me thinking about the meanings of motion and for sharing great conversation and many laughs. Thank you to Kevin, Keci, and Zarie Harvey, Dustin Miller, Jon Ball, Andrew Teska, Colby Jones, Zach Tooman, Graham Harding, and Richard Price Sensei for your support and encouragement. Carlos Sesia, visual artist and martial artist, deserves my deepest gratitude for exchange about visual and material expressions of space and time; I appreciate your intellect and kindness. I am truly grateful for the guidance and support of Andrew Sato Shihan; thank you, Sensei. Laura DeGraff Sensei, Dojo Cho of Kiku Matsu, helped me get unstuck at a crucial point in this research; your skills in aikido and information science are an inspiration. L. Teresa Church: thank you for your work and vision; I am grateful for our conversations. Dawn M. Burns, longtime fellow traveler, thank you for your friendship, support, and encouragement. Keep writing on trains, my friend.

I would be remiss to leave out gratitude for Rocky and Bullwinkle. Bullwinkle, who always knew the exact right time to drop a running shoe on my keyboard, and Rocky, who snored and farted through the writing of many drafts, reminded me that sometimes a good rest or a nice run makes for clearer thinking. This book took me so long that Rocky, your little face grayed during the process. Thank you for being a good friend.

Max and Ian: when I started this project, you were kids. Now you are adults, and I am so proud of you. I had the privilege of seeing you become more you as I worked on this project. You're fun and smart and kind. I love sharing my life with you, and traveling with you provided some of my best memories. I'm glad I took so many pictures. Thank you for making my life and work meaningful and rich.

This book started from a wanderlust that has been with me from birth and which had to express itself through library and museum visits when geographic isolation, economic limitations, and some of the cultural legacy of the mass production of memory led me to think that travel was for the rich only. Travel through my job changed that for me, as did additional insight into the social, economic, political, and cultural limitations placed on mobility in the past. This book then grew from a place of privilege as I got my first passport just before age forty. My current mobility privilege is shaped by race, class, gender, and nation in ways similar to and emerging from the privileges and inequities of the Age of the Kodak. Today, people seeking not just leisure through mobility but safety, security, family, and a means of self-support face incarceration at US borders, while others breeze past borders with the documents stamped by empire and the money to ensure the freedom and comfort of movement. I hope that insight into meaning making and travel in the past helps affirm physical movement as a fundamental human right today and fortifies our work to change policy and practice that limit this right and that are built on racism, classism, religious bigotry, and homophobia. People need freedom for movement and movement for freedom.

Coda: I finish this book during a global pandemic, trying to focus. As someone who spent the last five years studying the connections among mobility, memory, archives, and power, I find my skills inadequate for commenting meaningfully on the current sickness, displacement, border closures, and economic distress. Perhaps in the arc of time I will have processed enough of this experience to offer something helpful. A new generation of camera users, however, have spoken clearly and meaningfully as they document, broadcast, and confront the racism, classism, and homophobia shaping both public space and historical memory in the United States. Being with you to clarify our opposition to police abuse and to the monumental abuses of historical knowledge in public spaces has been an honor, as well as a fitting conclusion of my work on this book. Thank you for making history, young people.

The Mass Production of Memory

"THE STORY IS COMPLETE FOR ALL TIME"

Mass Photography for the Future of History

Between 1919 and 1951, civil rights activist, pioneering jurist, Episco-
palian priest, writer, and gender identity innovator Pauli Murray kept a
photo album. They documented activities at school, family in Durham,
North Carolina, and friends in New York.[1] The majority of the photos,
though, referenced travel, especially in the 1930s, a time when they began to openly experiment with identity. On the road, and despite the
restrictions of limited budget and the dangers of Jim Crow, they found
travel to be freeing, and in their travel photos and captions they referenced pride in technological mastery, an eagerness to explore, an open-
ness with people, and love for their partner at the time, Peggie Holmes.
They even included a page that attested to the many facets of their identity with a photo dedicated to each, like "The Imp" and "The Acrobat,"
and one they associated with travel, "The Vagabond," in which Murray
wore their preferred menswear style. The album was part of a massive
personal archive attesting to a life lived purposefully, courageously, and
richly, but it was an item that was visual and crafted to communicate a
self that was a work of art in continuous emergence. While Pauli Murray

1

did not look like or have the privileges of the white, fashionable, carefree "Kodak Girl" the Eastman Kodak Company imagined when designing its signature marketing figure for its innovative portable film camera, they used their camera as Kodak instructed in its marketing: they created a visual archive of their own experiences from their own perspective, making the most of the personal visual legacy machine.

Murray was not alone. When Kodak released the first workable, portable film camera in 1888, followed by its even more affordable version, the Brownie, in 1900, Americans embraced portable photography. The Kodaks, which enclosed the film in a box that could then be sent to Eastman Kodak for processing (eliminating the need for a darkroom), set off a wave of hobby photography and made photographic image creation a part of daily life in the United States. Emerging at the same time that Americans increasingly engaged in travel vacations, the Kodak became associated with leisure travel, in no small part because of the company's aggressive marketing efforts. In using their cameras on their trips, hobby photographers constructed collective memory and reworked their own relationships to the past and to the nation's narratives about the past. Not only did they use their cameras to make distinctions between their modern selves and the "quaint" scenes and people they experienced on their sightseeing trips, but also they began to see their photos as ways to enter the national narrative, to record history as they lived it. I call this phenomenon the mass production of memory not because I think that camera users created uniform memories with their cameras (although sometimes that happened), but because camera users participated in a system of mass consumption and production of images. They bought mass-produced cameras on a large scale, and in turn used them to produce visual evidence—photos and albums—mnemonic devices that would eventually make it to an archive, whether institutional or familial, where they would do the work of helping us understand the past.

In the late nineteenth and early twentieth centuries, when Americans strengthened their beliefs in individuals' power to determine personal and societal destiny through leisure travel, the camera on tour became a crucial tool of self-definition and group identity. During this time, however, Americans differed significantly in the challenges they faced in defining self and community. Prescriptions and proscriptions based on race, gender, class, nation, and sexuality profoundly affected how individuals moved about the country and the world. Some used travel and cameras to assert privilege, while others used the same to confront privilege and assert their own visibility. Systems of privilege also informed the archiving of the materials produced by the first generation to experience mass photography. This book tells the story of the camera's emerging centrality in leisure travel and its significant role in the mass production of memory, a process in which camera users created a vast visual archive attesting to their experiences, their values, and their circumstances. Today, a proliferation of accounts of tourist photography in newspapers and magazines, travel diaries, and letters referencing "Kodakery," business documents of the Eastman Kodak Company, and scores of albums and photos in archives and private collections large and small in the United States remain to attest to the popular association of travel with picture taking and to the social, political, economic, and cultural exigencies that shaped both activities.

Like media scholars today who seek to understand the role of social media companies in the production of memory, I focus on the influence of Kodak to analyze, in the words of communication scholars Rik Smit, Ansgard Heinrich, and Marcel Broersma in their study of the role of Facebook in the 2014 Ferguson, Missouri, protests, the "underlying mechanics" shaping the creation of memory, but unlike social media scholars, I am concerned with the structures of analog production and circulation.[2] By centralizing the white middle-class family in its aggressive advertising campaigns, its closed-loop system which encouraged consumer dependency, and its international reach which supported privileged consumer fantasies, the Eastman Kodak Company played a significant role in perpetuating the social inequities that informed claims to the public spaces of tourism, emphasizing the notion that the white middle class (and especially white women) should produce materials for performing contemporary social functions and ensuring future historical understanding. While both consumers and Kodak shaped the meanings of portable photography, the economic exigencies of mass consumption in a society stratified by race, class, and gender favored white middle-class consumers, who only rarely questioned their right and responsibility to create and command the nation's visual archive and their centrality in it. Through the mass production of memory and tourism, the company and its white middle-class consumers made powerful claims on public space that inform the meanings of place and the past to this day.

Photography, Memory, History

To sell cameras to tourists on a mass scale in the late nineteenth and early twentieth centuries, the Eastman Kodak Company needed to convince consumers that they were not up to the monumentality of remembering, and that without photos, their stories would be incomplete for the ages. Even more fundamentally, they had to be convinced that their experiences *deserved* documenting; that their children, their travels, their holidays, and even their service in the military were not just the bits and pieces of daily living but part of a national history worthy of recording, sharing, and committing to posterity. Particularly during World War I (an especially profitable time for the company), Kodak connected personal history to national history as a way to heighten the importance of individual experiences—experiences that would require a more scientific recording than the old-fashioned diary could provide. An ad cut for the autographic Kodak—the camera that allowed users to write a short phrase that would be exposed in the photo itself—featured American travelers in Europe and urged consumers to "Keep not merely the picture story of your travels but write the date and title on your every film . . . before you forget."[3] A 1922 ad in the *Saturday Evening Post* offered the camera as a loyal servant in the task of remembering: "The lens sees with you—the autographic record remembers for you—and the story is complete for all time."[4] This ad relied on the idea that personal memory could be as exacting as historical science with the right recording technology, despite the fact that the window that let users write on the film allowed for only about fifteen characters. Like a telegram, it had room for only the briefest messages.[5] It also responded to anxieties about progress; one could use the camera to record events before they inevitably changed. Another ad urged consumers to "Let Kodak save the day. Particularly at vacation time, there's so much you want to remember— and pictures won't let you forget. Kodak saves the day—for the years."[6] By the time this ad appeared, other companies were seeing Kodak's appeal to consumer anxieties over memory and preserving history for the future as a signature marketing approach. Writing in *Printer's Ink*, an advertising trade publication, C. B. Larrabee commented that the "big idea behind the selling of Eastman Kodaks is that every man can write the outline of his own history, and that the outline will be a hundredfold more interesting if it is illustrated."[7] About twenty years before American Historical Association president Carl L. Becker famously declared,

"Everyman His Own Historian," Kodak had made the idea a central marketing strategy.[8] With a camera, Kodak asserted, more people really could have their own individual impacts on the future's understanding of the past.

Kodak's customers answered the company's call to use its product to claim control over time with a similar claim to control over space. Camera users fashioned the world—sometimes directly and sometimes obliquely—as their own country of sorts, a "Camera-Land" constructed for their own edification and amusement. This phenomenon was informed by many middle- and upper-class Americans' emerging sense of themselves as a modern people distinct from the rest of the world, which, in their view, was clinging to the past. The mass-market-produced box camera connected the past to the future through the leisure economy, and did so in two ways. First, American tourists' preference for photographic subjects representing the past—cemeteries, historic houses, historic landscapes, monuments—revealed the role of historical memory in the growth of both photography and mass travel. Second, camera users' preference for people-in-place shots demonstrated their desire to create a personal archive that would eventually enter the national narrative.

In the context of heightened meaning for both consumerism and experience, memory and its democratizing relationship to the construction of history had become both mass-produced and marketable. This process, which took shape in the four decades following the introduction of the portable Kodak, fed into a renewed interest in heritage, for the individual's responsibility to shape one's world extended to one's past as well. In the Progressive Era, a strengthened cultural emphasis on individuals' opportunities and duties to shape their worlds as they saw fit fed into the association of the camera with travel. Wealthier heterosexual white Americans, buoyed by camera marketing that pictured them as fashionable and technologically sophisticated people, made implicit and explicit attempts to justify white privilege through both travel and the use of cameras by pointing their lenses at the people and places they considered primitive. New opportunities for personal recording magnified the importance of personal archiving and created new obligations for an accounting of oneself; one's status, ambitions, values, and personality could—and should—be preserved for assessment by others both in the present and in the future. In taking up newly available techniques for personal expression through travel and the display of associated mementos, tourist photographers fit into a system of status production and surveillance, a dynamic proposed by Shawn Michelle Smith in 1999 in *American Archives*.[9] In providing a mass of Americans with the tools for controlling one's future assessment by historians, Kodak made its consumers' private lives more public through the mass production of memory.

Americans, though, experienced the mass production of memory in different ways. While white photographers, publishers, and scientists employed the camera in ways that promoted stereotypes of people of color, poor people of all backgrounds, and sexual minorities, individuals from these groups used their own photographs and albums, as well as their own behavior in front of whites wielding cameras, to subvert these stereotypes. In the first period in US history that saw mass photographic recording, African Americans fought against the entrenchment of Jim Crow, institutionalized white violence, and diverse attempts at limiting their mobility and right to self-definition. For Native people, this period marked continued assaults on their freedom via the reservation system and harassment from both settlers and the military enacting federal policies. It also brought new attacks on Native culture through the boarding school movement and the criminalization of language, religious observance, and other cultural practices. Growing gay communities in cities operated spaces of leisure designed to enable freer sexual expression; dance clubs, hotels, and beach areas supported community life, which participants sometimes documented photographically. Such documentation evidenced a desire to preserve moments of freedom in a dominant society that was becoming increasingly hostile to those outside the tradition of a heteronormative male-female binary. African Americans, American Indians, and sexual minorities embraced the opportunity presented by the camera as a new technology of self-definition and documented their experiences in ways that confronted powerful attempts to limit them to visual stereotypes. Members of these communities, however different from one another, participated in the mass practices of tourism and photography, thereby producing rich visual archives. The inequities of access to public space, however, limited full expression of mobility in the visual record. Despite these limits and the Eastman Kodak Company's call to individual documentation which privileged middle-class whiteness, people who faced limits on their access to public space found new ways to embrace leisure, travel, and photography.

Ubiquity Is Not Banality

Scholars of US history in the age of the Kodak paid attention to the relationships among power, historical understanding, and the image. Leading them was the intellectual historian Ralph Henry Gabriel, who promoted the image as a primary source for historical understanding as well as an ideal method for communicating historical themes to audiences outside academia. He edited the series "The Pageant of America: A Pictorial History of the United States," which brought together leading scholars to discuss the major themes in American history through the image. Yale University Press published the series from 1925 to 1929 as part of the commemoration of the 150th anniversary of the country's founding.[10] Part coffee table book, part historical monograph, and part travelogue, the series presented the United States in a historical and geographic panorama, linking history with movement through space as well as time. The photograph as a historical event saw a resurgence of scholarly interest more recently with the publication of Alan Trachtenberg's *Reading American Photographs* in 1989, and historians have produced a sizable body of work attesting to the power of photography in the growth of visual culture. This was a conversation started in the humanities by Roland Barthes in *Camera Lucida* in 1980 and by Susan Sontag in *On Photography* in 1977.[11] Scholarly interest in the Kodak Company increased with the growth of literature on photography. Nancy Martha West focused more specifically on the historical context for mass photography in her look at Kodak marketing and established an important association between marketing and the growth of nostalgia as a cultural practice enacted through mass photography.[12] *Kodak Girl: From the Martha Cooper Collection* made materials related to women and photography more widely available and at the same time emphasized the importance of the camera in women's history: women as photographers, photographic subjects, and advertising images.[13] More broadly, scholars have also looked at the role of the camera and the photograph in negotiating power relations, particularly through race and gender in the United States. In *American Archives*, Shawn Michelle Smith analyzed turn-of-the-twentieth-century visual culture in terms of power relations, identifying important connections between white women's subjectivity and white privilege, including an observation of the similarities between eugenicist thinking and family photos.[14] Following Deborah Willis's significant body of work, including *Reflections in Black* and White: A History of Black Photographers, 1840 to Present, she and other scholars demonstrated the central role of photographers and photographs in African American political and cultural lives and community-building efforts during the nineteenth and early twentieth centuries.[15] The scholars of Indigenous photography Hulleah Tsinhnahjinnie, Amy Lonetree, and Mique'l Askren Dangeli analyze Native uses of photography in the past and assert the significant role of photos in maintaining community resilience in the present.[16] Malcolm Andrews's study The Search for the Picturesque: Landscape Aesthetics and Tourism in Britain, 1760–1800 was one of the first to explore the connection between tourism (in this case nature tourism) and photography.[17] Other scholars looked at photography and tourism as part of a complex of ethnographic and ethnocentric practices in the late nineteenth and early twentieth centuries.[18]

In the last half century, as scholars produced rich new bodies of work examining photography, historians and geographers have increased our understanding of tourism. Historians have been particularly active in analyzing the role of tourism in the maintenance and/or replication of imperial relations, tourism's role in nation building or international relations, and tourism as cultural capital.[19] In recent years, scholars have looked at ways in which people of the past used the camera to understand their heritage, such as Elizabeth Edwards in her work on the record photography movement in England around the turn of the twentieth century.[20] While this approach has not been applied specifically to understanding the history of tourism, it has the potential to yield a great deal of information about the role photography played in the development of tourism, in particular the role of the camera and the ways tourists used it to construct historical memory in shaping its contours.

Theorists of memory have engaged the relationship between individual and collective memory in ways that are instructive for understanding mass portable photography. The sociologist Maurice Halbwachs observed in 1950 (in a book published after his murder at Buchenwald in 1945) that memory makes sense only when articulated through community, effectively fusing individual memory and collective memory. He examined religion, the family, and social classes as structures in this formation.[21] More recently, the cultural theorists Jan Assmann and John Czaplicka further explicated the relationship, emphasizing the generative qualities of the connections between individual and collective memory in identity formation.[22] Alison Landsberg's theory of prosthetic memory provides an important framework for understanding the role of mass culture in collective memory. She argues compellingly that mass culture—particularly print and film—provided an opportunity for historical empathy, the chance for consumers of culture to identify with a group history that is not in the lived experience of the consumer or his or her family or community history. Landsberg notes the political potential of mass culture to encourage identification outside one's own social milieu.[23] Her thesis is important to the present work for illuminating the power of mass culture in collective memory. Barbie Zelizer's work on the mass consumption of journalistic images of the Holocaust showed that photography profoundly shaped public memory of that event by giving viewers a common language, but it also a had ubiquity that facilitated erasure.[24] While cinema and print media permeated the boundaries of group identity to encourage empathy (or, in some cases, willful amnesia), photography as a mass medium generated by the consumer presents a unique case. This book builds on Landsberg's groundbreaking work by examining vernacular photography as a form of mass media in which the consumers are also the producers. Camerists bought Kodaks and film, accessed lessons from the Kodak Company via advertising and instruction manuals, relied on developing services set up in an international network, but produced photos that represented their own individual experiences.

Whereas cinema or print media, as Landsberg shows, encouraged understanding across groups, personal photos encouraged individuation, atomizing memory in ways that cinema and print media did not. The generative properties of mass photography made culture customizable. Even though touring camerists visited many of the same places, stayed at many of the same hotels, and even took photos that looked alike, they developed photos and shared them with others as their own unique experiences. They consumed cameras, but they produced individualized memories on a large scale, which is why I refer to the process as the mass production of memory; that is, while the memories may have been individualized, the photography became a mass practice. Hobby photography was like the scrapbook hobby Ellen Gruber Garvey describes in *Writing with Scissors: American Scrapbooks from the Civil War to the Harlem Renaissance*. Garvey demonstrates that Americans embraced scrapbooks as a response to the abundance of information available in print, a method for processing and reordering information in ways that made sense to the individuals producing the books. She also shows the scrapbook to be an analog antecedent to current personal digital information management practices.[25] Like scrapbooks, vernacular travel photography allowed camerists to order information, but unlike scrapbooks as a whole, tourists photos allowed users to organize place. The roots of today's customizable, atomized cultural practices may also be found in the first generation of portable photography as Garvey has shown those roots in scrapbooks. Consumers could participate in a generative mass practice but with their own intonations, preferences, and views of the people and places around them. Mass portable photography made possible by the Kodak was one dress rehearsal for Web 2.0.

Since the publication of John Urry's study *The Tourist Gaze*, scholars have made much of the power of the tourist through his or her act of looking. But tourist photos also reveal the tourist as someone to be gazed upon. Through self-presentation in the photograph, the tourist becomes the object of the gaze and points to others looking upon the tourist, a dynamic that Urry's later analysis acknowledged.[26] Like the Grand Tourist's portrait which revealed a desire to evoke the past for present power, the tourist photo from a later period has the potential to reveal the social, economic, political, and cultural meanings of the past as understood through leisure travel. Yet historians have largely overlooked photos taken by tourists, as well as the marketing items, newspaper coverage, diaries, letters, and magazine buzz centered on "Kodakery," as evidence of the complex relationships among mobility, photographic technologies, and self-definition through personal documentation, archiving, and other activities that shaped historical memory. My work engages this material in a context of power relations—social, political, economic, and national—that shaped new meanings for one's image in the late nineteenth and early twentieth centuries.

The functions of large corporations with international reach in collective memory is a central concern of this work. A transactional social contract made tourist photography possible on a mass scale. The Eastman Kodak Company provided the equipment, the technical training, and a sociocultural lens through which to document one's experiences and share them with other people. Consumers bought in to the Kodak system, on which they largely depended for developing film and making prints. The effects of Kodak's massive, integrated, and innovative marketing campaigns—the sociocultural part of the contract—are less easily documented. Consumers often produced photos that looked like the ones Kodak taught them to make, but they often did not, for their lives did not always look like the images of the white, middle-class, heteronormative families that appeared in Kodak's ads. The images were frequently more irreverent and much less polished (and many badly framed and poorly lit!). While consumers largely fulfilled the technical and economic parts of the social contract by choosing to purchase Kodaks and use them, they departed from the company's messages about the identity they should reflect and create through the personal legacy machine. Interestingly, Kodak's advertising—which was ubiquitous on a scale comparable at the time to that of Pond's or Philip Morris—rarely shared what the photos were supposed to look like, and instead centralized images that showed what the consumer was supposed to look like or feel like while taking the photos. Their famous early but long-lasting tagline "You press the button; we do the rest" implied a caregiving relationship between corporation and consumer. "The rest," however, went way beyond photo development and far into identity development for both individuals and groups: consumer-producers did the work of making meaning and generating an archive. The paternal corporation may have enabled the process, but it certainly could not control it; the "children" proved they could be unruly.

In this work, I have taken care to seek out the albums and photos of people who differed demographically from the consumer demographics Kodak's marketing assumed, for they operated their cameras in social situations set up to limit their participation in public space and culture. The circumstances for both tourism and personal archiving existed in distinction from the norm as established by the corporation and dominant society, and so their case studies reveal some of the nuances and limits of the social contract enabling the mass production of memory. While this volume examines the photos and albums of individuals with multiple and diverse community associations and identity markers, it is not a focused study of any one community; rather, it is an examination of the ways in which individuals of many demographic characteristics—place, ethnicity, race, gender and sexual identification, class, religion—participated in the growth of two related mass phenomena, tourism and photography, which shaped modern understandings of the past. While many people took photos while traveling in the period from 1880 to 1930, individuals accessed these activities according to the parameters of their participation in public spaces, which were often determined by markers of identity and community. An economically disenfranchised, queer African American woman had a radically different relationship to the public spaces of tourism than did a wealthy white heterosexual man, and even though both may have taken photos while traveling, their mobility and public behaviors—both crucial to tourist photography—were circumscribed in different ways, and hence their tourist photos and albums resonated differently and took on different meanings. Native peoples regularly faced white violence, both on and off reservations. Gay men experimenting with gendered looks in cities faced homophobic violence outside their own communities. These examples demonstrate radically different relationships to public spaces than those of white, richer, gender-conforming people, and hence affected tourist photography and the historical records produced by it. People privileged with mobility and safety often produced tourist photos that looked more like landscape paintings or ethnographic studies. Those whose mobility and participation in communal public space was monitored or limited by the dominant society produced photos and albums that centered closely on community or loved ones rather than on widely focused views. Restrictions on individual mobility and safety produced a historical record of communities crafting their own images, photos to be shared within the group that experienced similar limits. It is my hope that this book will provide an analysis that facilitates more detailed future studies of the functions of tourist and family photography in the shaping of historical memory in individual communities.

Mass tourism, mass photography, and the marketing of both grew unevenly in the late nineteenth and early twentieth centuries as different individuals embraced these practices for similar purposes but with different resonances; all, however, spoke to a strengthening imperative to produce, and thereby control, the materials available to those in the future who would be assessing the past. The mass production of memory depended on mass concern about the future. While camera use and leisure travel grew steadily overall, more privileged citizens gained better access to both activities and established expectations for tourist photography, given that systems of race and class privilege positioned them as those with the education, means, and savvy to control the power of mobility and technology. Gender played an interesting role in the establishment of photographic privilege, as white middle-class women had a special role in the popular conception of cameras as tools for remembrance; in the prescriptive literature, they took on increasing centrality as culture keepers. Chapter 1, "'One did not 'take' a camera': The Roots of Tourist Photography," examines the origins of tourist photography in painting and lithography that replicated some of the themes of the Grand Tour of the eighteenth century. Chapter 2, "'The World is mine—I own a KODAK': Marketing Memory and Privilege," analyzes the marketing of cameras to tourists with an emphasis on portability and technological mastery, an association that wed the camera to the act of travel by establishing both as central to the power of whiteness and economic freedom. The Eastman Kodak Company, the largest manufacturer of cameras and film in the early twentieth century, implemented an ambitious and diverse marketing plan that set the tone for the association of camera use with both mobility and privilege, but its images did not always reflect the realities of camera use. Chapter 3, "'Side Trips in Camera-Land': Tourism and the Visual Record," explores public dialogue about personal recording by the first generation of tourist photographers. This dialogue amplified the modernity of the camera user and shaped photographic habits around personal memory and family needs. Chapter 4, "'When I Send You a Picture of Berlin': The Memory Emergency of the First World War," explores the increasing use of cameras during World War I and the heightened fears of failing to record for posterity. By separating families and endangering lives, World War I increased the personal documentation and archiving imperative initiated by earlier leisure travel. Both Kodak in its marketing and individuals in their personal photographs drew on touristic forms of documentation in an attempt to deal with the perplexities and traumas of war. Chapter 5, "'A visible token': Expanding the Promise of the Kodak in the Interwar Years," demonstrates that Americans drew heavily on the promise of the camera for individual identity creation as mobility increased in the period between the wars. Cars sometimes allowed circumnavigation around restrictions on public behavior for women, Native Americans, African Americans, and gay, lesbian, and transgender individuals and informed the making and saving of vacation snaps. While these communities had significant internal diversities, individuals within each faced similar conditions affecting mobility, access to technology, and safety. These exigencies shaped recording behaviors and complicated the messages provided by Kodak marketing. In these cases, the photograph operated as a witness to history in the making and encouraged community documentation and family archiving. A concluding chapter, "The Legacy of the First Generation of Mass Tourism and Portable Photography," examines this period of intense photographic and travel activity in terms of photographic and touristic behaviors and their implications for historians, archivists, curators, museum educators, and historic site managers as well as social media users.

When people took photographs of their leisure travels in the late nineteenth and early twentieth centuries, they meant their photos and albums to convey a variety of messages: I am adventurous/worldly/committed to family. I am wealthy enough to be temporarily in a space not my own. I am superior to those without personal recording technology. My history is important. My family and community are prospering. I want to share something about myself with you. I want to take control of my own image. On the surface, such declarations seem rather timeless, or even existential. But the first generation to experiment with mass portable photography did so in a context of power relations specific to that time, an era with inequalities and contradictions that helped to shape contemporary public photographic behaviors. The Kodak Company asserted that everyone's history deserved preservation through the ages, a "story complete for all time," and even though their "everyone" was limited to those most likely to afford cameras, many people took the camera manufacturer's promise at face value. While some Americans used the camera and geographic mobility to try to naturalize power relations based on class, nation, gender, and race, others employed them to confront the denial of their humanity in the context of increasing homophobia, institutionalized white supremacy, and ongoing genocide. For these reasons, historians must not mistake the ubiquity of the tourist photograph for banality.

"ONE DID NOT 'TAKE' A CAMERA"

The Roots of Tourist Photography

Americans used travel and cameras to represent their identities on the basis of visual culture carried over from an earlier period. Heritage had been a motivation for travel in the modern era since the popularization of the Grand Tour, a phenomenon that started in the sixteenth century and peaked in the eighteenth century, and visual culture had been associated with it from the beginning. Grand Tourists, usually young men of means primarily from England, took extensive tours of Europe, with a particular focus on Italy. The purpose of the tour was to provide classical learning in art and architecture as well as lessons in the aristocratic manners of the Continent. Self-presentation with relics of the past was also a part of the Grand Tour tradition. Grand Tourists hired painters to create portraits that included the visual evidence of history—ruins, artworks, books—to present themselves as heirs to the power of Roman and Greek antiquity.[1] Artifacts and authority aligned in the visual culture of the Grand Tour. For instance, Pompeo Batoni (1708–87), the most popular Italian painter of tourist portraits, painted over two hundred portraits of British travelers from around 1740 to the end of his life. While only about a quarter of them evoked antiquity, these attracted a great deal of attention from patrons and collectors.[2] In the 1750s, the young James Caulfield, who would become the first Earl of Charlemont, paused in his seven-year-long journey through Europe and the Middle East to pose for a Batoni portrait. While his lavish clothing attested to his wealth, the view of the Roman Colosseum through a window over his shoulder attested to the cultural capital accrued through heritage tourism.[3] The subject of another Batoni portrait, Sir Wyndham Knatchbull-Wyndham, points observers toward his own view of a historical landscape (figure 1). In 1764, Edward Augustus posed for Batoni, who repeated the composition of the stately man gesturing past a powerfully large column toward the Colosseum.[4] William Gordon, military man and aristocratic tourist, raised the political stakes of the relationship between past and present power in 1766 by posing in exquisite Scottish military regalia while surrounded by Roman artifacts, including the Colosseum and a monument to a Roman deity.[5] As the British middle class grew in the nineteenth century, its members gained increased exposure to Grand Tour paintings through the tradition of house tours, a ritual described by Jane Austen in *Pride and Prejudice* when she narrates Elizabeth Bennet's visit to Mr. Darcy's estate with her upper-middle-class aunt and uncle.[6] Batoni's portraits of English travelers speak to the established tradition of self-documentation and evocation of the past while on tour, a tradition continued by these travelers' camera-holding descendants. The Grand Tour roots of tourist photography fed into the idea that travel and the visual evidence of it were the responsibility of the privileged—defined especially in terms of race and class—whose experiences could then be used as justification for their social position. Visual evidence of travel was cultural capital.

As mass travel increased in the nineteenth century and a specialized tourist industry developed in tandem, American travelers continued some of the traditions of the earlier Grand Tour. They visited ruins, museums, and galleries, and took pride in relating these experiences to their social set when they returned home. Starting around 1870, photos of them, usually produced by professional photographers hired on-site or brought with the touring parties, featured not just the ruins of the world but the tourists posing among them, just as Batoni's sitters had emphasized their status as heirs to power. Professional photos of tourists among ruins implied control over space, and the presence of relics also implied control over time in the form of historical memory. The people-in-historic-places photos showed that the tourist had not only

Figure 1. A souvenir of the Grand Tour. Pompeo Batoni,
Portrait of Sir Wyndham Knatchbull-Wyndham, 1758–1759.
Original oil on canvas, housed at the Los Angeles County Museum of Art.

the means and leisure to travel to Europe but also the refinement to appreciate antiquities.

Modern travel clothes, casual poses, and sometimes the very modern presence of another camera created a visual distinction between the tourists and the evidence of the past civilizations that surrounded them. Such a distinction betrayed the ambivalence many Americans felt toward antiquities; as citizens of a relatively new nation focused on invention and economic development, American travelers of the upper middle class tended to identify with powerful past civilizations that embodied their ambitions, but at the same time they wanted to see themselves as a people focused on progress. An example from literature—*Innocents Abroad* by Mark Twain—demonstrated Americans' anxiety over their own interest in the past. In 1867 Twain set out upon a steamer cruise of the Mediterranean to experience the history and culture of the region. *Innocents Abroad*, a parody of the sentimental travel narrative so popular in his time, resulted from this trip, and it included a passage on touring the art and ruins of Rome. Fatigued from "wander[ing] among the crumbling wonders" and being "fed upon the dust and decay of five-and-twenty centuries," its narrator worries that he might turn into a ruin himself and be "liable at any moment to fall a prey to some antiquary and be patched in the legs, and 'restored' with an unseemly nose, and labeled wrong and dated wrong, and set up in the Vatican for poets to drivel about and vandals to scribble their names on forever and forevermore."[7] Twain's narrator satirizes the project of preservation and the creation of a material archive, particularly its social pretensions and the graffiti those pretensions invited. Even though the narrator never takes a photo or commissions a painting of his image on tour, he worries about becoming a pathetic remnant of history in the future.[8]

The tension between what Twain saw as the detritus of the past and the needs of the tourist to appear modern was symbolically resolved with photography. By posing with the ruins of the past and conveying the resulting images through photographic technologies such as lantern slides, the stereoscope, and the album, American tourists echoed their relatively new nation's tentative claims to the power of empire. Recreating a visual narrative similar to that advanced by Pompeo Batoni and his eighteenth-century sitters, they established their own connection to empires past. With the camera, though, tourists could lay claim to the past and at the same time assert their distinction from it as modern people with contemporary recording technology.

While the more elite international American tourists in Europe used visual culture to engage issues of national power, a wider variety of tourists traveled domestically. As travel narratives and other cultural products made normative the white upper-middle-class leisure tourist, Americans of different social and economic positions found ways to travel that departed from the model of the two-week to two-month leisure tour. Middle- and working-class American travelers differed from their more elite counterparts in that they were in the process of overcoming their suspicion of leisure. Cindy Aron's work on public dialogue about vacations for the American middle and working classes reveals much angst about free time; Americans worried that idleness among the middle classes could erode the work ethic that served as part of the foundation of republicanism.[9] This angst led to the development of "productive" vacationing, trips devoted to increasing one's knowledge (as in the case of Chautauquas), promoting health through agricultural labor, working vacations, revivals and religious retreats, and sightseeing.[10] Among these, sightseeing was the most popular way to vacation and at the same time feel productive. Nineteenth-century vacationers could set an agenda of sights to see and experiences to have and then busy themselves visiting natural wonders like Niagara Falls, wild landscapes, and even institutions like asylums and prisons. Cemeteries and battlefields were special venues to visit and in which to talk about the past.[11] Travelers exploring the new places to which their work led them could visit sites in short day trips in between periods of work. Artists, salesmen, entertainers, and teachers were among the travelers who combined work and tourism. By the late nineteenth century, as shown by the historian Marguerite S. Shaffer, domestic tourism offered Americans a way to shape their national identity as a people possessing both landscapes comparable in magnitude to the most magnificent cathedrals of Europe and the sense to appreciate these American scenes of grandeur.[12]

Photography fit neatly into the American style of productive tourism, but it was bulky and technical in the 1870s. The photos that tourists brought home before the advent of the Kodak in 1888 were likely the product of a professional hired for the occasion.[13] The experience of being photographed was part of the excitement of the vacation, as depicted in James Wells Champney's illustration "The Season at Niagara Falls," which appeared in *Harper's* in 1877. It depicts a serene couple being photographed in front of the grandeur of Niagara Falls, but the scene outside the frame of the camera is chaotic: onlookers, unruly dogs, busy children (figure 2). Photography was not so much a hobby, as it would become later, as it was itself an event. Tourists in this era could also buy prepared albums created by professional photographers showing popular views of the architecture, features, and people of the places they visited. Unlike the later amateur photo albums, these minimized the presence of the tourist in the photos themselves.[14]

When Champney drew "The Season at Niagara Falls" in 1877, tourist photography needed some modernizing, and George Eastman was working on the problem. In 1872, the young Eastman was one of the few intrepid tourists trying with difficulty to take his own photos; unlike others, he successfully improved the cumbersome technology. Carl Ackerman, who wrote the only full-length biography of Eastman published during his lifetime, recounted Eastman's photographic experiments while traveling and noted that Eastman took his first trip to Niagara Falls as part of a tour of the East Coast. Upon his return to Rochester, he "spent more time at his workbench" perfecting his photographic ideas.[15] On another trip, Eastman noted that his "photographic outfit" was hard to carry: "I bought an outfit and learned that it took not only a strong but a dauntless man to be an outdoor photographer. My layout, which included only the essentials, had in it a camera about the size of a soap box, a tripod, which was strong and heavy enough to support a bungalow, a big plate-holder, a dark-tent, a nitrate bath, and a container for water." Additionally, developing materials were difficult to transport, which he reported to Ackerman, saying: "The nitrate of silver was something that always had to go along and it was perhaps the most awkward companion imaginable on a journey. . . . The first time I took a silver bath away with me, I wrapped it with exceeding great care and put it in my trunk. The cover leaked, the nitrate got out, and stained most of my clothing." Eastman summarized his early travels with a camera by saying that "in those days, one did not 'take' a camera, one accompanied the outfit of which the camera was only a part. . . . It seemed that one ought to be able to carry less than a pack-horse load."[16]

In addition to learning firsthand about the unwieldiness of cameras, Eastman had another early experience that taught him an important feature of tourist photography: the presence of a camera shaped the experience of tourism itself and led people to behave differently than if the camera were not present. In his early travels, Eastman had "become wholly absorbed in photography—in spite of all the trouble involved and in spite of the fact that, whenever I set up my apparatus, a crowd drew

Figure 2. James Wells Champney, "The Season at Niagara Falls,"
Harper's Weekly, August 18, 1877 (Harpweek).

around as though I were going to open a patent-medicine show." In the 1870s, he tried to take a photograph of a natural wonder but ended up causing a commotion with the presence of his camera:

> One burning hot day I set up my encampment to go about photographing the natural bridge at Mackinac. . . . [A] party of tourists . . . draped themselves about the bridge engaging attitudes that were then thought necessary when one was photographed close to nature. I paid no attention to them, took several exposures, and when I had finished, one of the men came forward and inquired the price. I told him that I was an amateur making pictures for my own amusement and not for sale. He exploded "Then why did you let us stand in the hot sun for a full half-hour while you fooled around with your contraptions!"[17]

Eastman learned that tourists—even in the early stages of the development of tourist photography—knew, from experience with professional photographers, the albums of their peers, and the visual traditions associated with genteel travel, the "appropriate" poses for demonstrating their place in a picturesque landscape. While he did not turn these tourists into customers that day, he had found a significant customer base for his later work and a foundation for building a marketing strategy that centralized leisure travel.

By the 1890s, George Eastman's company had tapped into touristic interest in photography and successfully addressed the portability and processing problems faced by traveling amateur photographers. The Kodak, a name Eastman gave his new portable camera because he thought it sounded "euphonious and snappy," became available in 1888.[18] It used a film roll system enclosed in a small box, and it came with an innovative business model as well: instead of having to maintain a darkroom, Kodak users simply sent the camera to a dealer for film developing and printing. The camera was then reloaded with film, and both camera and photo prints were sent back to the customer. By 1900, Frank Brownwell, a designer at the company, had fulfilled Eastman's request to come up with an even more scaled-down model of the Kodak which put photography within the means of almost everyone. The "Brownie," the Model-T of cameras, was a standardized version that cost one dollar. Six exposures could be developed for fifteen cents, and a roll of film cost forty cents.[19] Eastman's invention had solved the portability issue for all camera users. Yet it was particularly important for tourists, who by definition depended on mobility and whose experiences were different from their home lives and therefore called for a way to remember them. The Kodak, and especially the Brownie, was a major step forward in the development of mass photography and the mass production of memory.

Mass production and the growth of consumer society in the latter half of the nineteenth century profoundly changed many American habits. More Americans were able to buy more things and fill their homes with carpets, furniture, books, and art that expressed their tastes, status, and identities.[20] As textiles manufacturing hit new production heights, fashionable clothing became more widely available, as did beauty and grooming products.[21] Rural delivery and catalog shopping ensured that consumer imperatives reached even the remotest of communities.[22] New appliances offered convenience, novelty, and, in the words of the historian of consumerism Charles F. McGovern, seemingly "universal access to luxury."[23] The portable camera, as a device that one could carry to visibly demonstrate one's fashion sense, technological savvy, and modernity and at the same time employ to document and share one's experiences, had a special and important place among the pantheon of new and improved consumer items. As a personal legacy machine, it could speak for the user long after the user had passed on, in a voice much more compelling than that of other consumer goods that would become inheritance items. Like a written diary of previous centuries, it could provide the future with insight into individual experiences. Unlike diaries, however, photos and albums spoke the more modern language of the visual, a language that would increase in importance throughout the twentieth century via advertising, film, magazines, and eventually television. It was a mass-produced item that allowed consumers to generate new products: pictures that represented their own experiences. While it was definitely a consumer good that allowed the owner a claim to class status, it was also a tool for production, extending productive capacity beyond the factory into the hands of consumers.

Improvements in transportation technologies meant that at the same time Americans began to buy portable film cameras, tourism and vacations became more accessible. The growing network of railroads in the last quarter of the nineteenth century brought remote places closer just as some employers decided that periodic vacations could improve the morale of employees and make them more productive. They targeted white-collar workers first and later extended the practice to some blue-collar workers.[24] Steamships had a similar effect on overseas travel, particularly to Europe, as well-to-do Americans increasingly sought meaning and status from Old World visits.[25] In the first few decades of the twentieth century, automobiles became financially within reach of middle-class and some working-class Americans, facilitating yet another wave of interest in mobility, vacations, and tourism. Thus transportation and recording technologies worked in tandem to create a new culture of personal archiving. Travelers did not have to satisfy themselves with merely telling the stories of their travels, as a previous generation had done. Now they could offer images as witness to their experiences of mobility and modernity. In the last decade of the nineteenth century and the first three decades of the twentieth, many Americans picked up their cameras and headed out their doors to visually document their individual experiences of family, community, country, and, increasingly, the rest of the world. The growth of mobility paired with the growth of leisure time to create a historical moment in which those who could afford even a bit of both took every opportunity to do so.

Chapter Two

"THE WORLD IS MINE—
I OWN A KODAK"
Marketing Memory and Privilege

Twenty-four years after its 1888 introduction of the first affordable, practical, portable handheld film camera, the Eastman Kodak Company dominated the amateur photography market. In that year, 1912, an ad in *Ladies' Home Journal* promoted its now widely owned camera, featuring a woman in a travel coat carrying a Kodak and standing on a train platform while literally looking down at an African American porter placing her multi-stickered, much-traveled suitcase on the platform (figure 3). The female subject in the ad, headed "The World is mine," has a decidedly erect bearing, the column of her traveling coat making her appear resolute and commanding. The porter's posture at the moment the suitcase hits the platform evokes a deferential bow. The class and race privilege promoted by the image is unmistakable, while the text reinforces the idea that the Kodak consumer has the power to order the world as she wants to see it: "Take a Kodak with *you*, and picture, from your own viewpoint, not merely the places that interest you but also the companions who help make your trip enjoyable."[1]

While neither the first nor the last association Eastman Kodak would make between travel and cameras, this ad is remarkable for the visual explicitness of its message about power. Command of technology, paired with geographic mobility, in the logic of the visual, translated directly to possession and control of space as well as race and class privilege. It forwarded the idea that Kodak consumers were a recording class, a group whose experiences and perspectives—particularly travel—were important enough to warrant documentation.

A closer examination of Kodak's broader marketing strategies of this period reveals some temporal nuances in the construction of this privilege, for the company used tourism to claim for its consumers the power to control future understandings of history. Throughout its early years, Kodak's marketing closely affiliated picture taking with travel, depicting camera users at exotic locations, in cars, on trains and train platforms, asserting that "a vacation without a Kodak is a vacation wasted." The company, with its hefty advertising budget (by 1900 it led the nation in advertising expenditure) and carefully cultivated advertising program, made expensive attempts at controlling the meaning of tourism and its potential for interactions that privileged the Kodak consumer and by extension the Kodak Company.[2] A temporal reading of its ads reveals that the power negotiated through touristic practices depended as much on camera users' ideas about past and present as on spatial constructs such as nation. In Kodak's marketing, cameras and albums created a temporal-visual complex in which tourists claimed power based on access to the tools that could record—and therefore control—future historical understanding. In this complex, the Kodak Company encouraged the conflation of history as the scientific record of the nation-state with personal and/or family memory, which tied the interests of individual consumers to the interests of the nation-state. From 1888, when the first Kodak was introduced, to the 1932 death of the company's founder, the Eastman Kodak Company's advertising grew bolder about asserting the duty of American camera consumers to record history. These ads reflected Kodak's appreciation of consumer dreams of class and imperial power and were part of the central role that the leisure economy broadly, and the heritage touristic trade more specifically, played in promoting the white American middle class as those who should control the meaning of history in a new, visually ordered world. Privilege rested on access to both cameras and travel; by the end of the First World War, Kodak advertising combined individual and transnational themes that

"*The World is mine—*
I own a KODAK"

Take a Kodak with *you*, and picture, from your own viewpoint, not merely the places that interest you but also the companions who help to make your trip enjoyable.

Anybody can take good pictures with a Kodak. Catalogue free at the dealers or by mail.

EASTMAN KODAK COMPANY,
ROCHESTER, N. Y., *The Kodak City.*

Figure 3.
"The World is mine,"
Kodak advertisement, 1912,
Emergence of Advertising in
America Collection, John W.
Hartman Center for Sales,
Advertising, and Marketing
History, Rubenstein Library,
Duke University.

functioned explicitly to centralize the camera as the most important actor in the construction of historical understanding and implicitly as a tool for enacting white privilege and class privilege.

Increasing access to travel—especially travel abroad—supported the popularity of the camera as a device to record tourist experience. Steam engine innovations of the latter half of the nineteenth century made travel accessible to more Americans, who used the railways and steamships to get away from home temporarily. While still a practice of the relatively privileged (working-class Americans would not start expecting vacations until the early twentieth century), touring became more widespread.[3] The economic historians Brandon Dupont, Alka Gandhi, and Thomas Weiss found that by the outbreak of the First World War, almost 250,000 Americans spent time outside the United States that year, a number that had risen 5.3 percent a year between 1820 and 1900.[4] The actual numbers deemphasize the effect of travel on American culture in the nineteenth century, for tourism provided the content for a literary outpouring of travel narratives and guidebooks eagerly consumed by Americans who may or may not have traveled themselves. William W. Stowe found that the educated elite and those aspiring to that status used travel books and guidebooks as a way to "claim social and professional positions for themselves, to gratify their desires for pleasure and especially for prestige, and to justify their privileges by demonstrating their superior taste and sensitivity."[5] By the turn of the twentieth century, Americans had a solid tradition of conflating tourism with power, and by the eve of the First World War, as Christopher Endy has shown, tourism was having significant effects on diplomatic decisions.[6]

In the late nineteenth and early twentieth centuries, tourists could record their part in this power dynamic with new film cameras that were portable and easy for amateurs to use, for they did not require the use of a darkroom, and Kodak featured this in its marketing. The first Kodak ad's tagline claimed, "You press the button—we do the rest," and the company lived up to that promise by not just selling cameras but developing photos and reloading film. Eastman matched the innovation of film technology with an innovative business model and marketing, building a network of local dealers in the United States and Europe to sell cameras and supplies and develop film. The national company, for its part, not only supplied dealers but also led an aggressive national marketing campaign and supported local dealers with information on products, selling tips, and notice of resources for local advertising through its monthly *Kodak Trade Circular*.[7] In the inaugural issue in December 1899, the circular outlined the national company's relationship to the dealer: "We believe that we are the only manufacturers of photographic goods who deliberately turn over to the dealer the difference between the retail and wholesale price. We have thus made ourselves dependent upon the dealer and the dealer upon us. Our relations are reciprocal; our interests identical." In that spirit, the circular's motto emphasized it was "for your interests and our own."[8] The circulars outlined a diverse marketing strategy, including postcards, posters, window displays, streetcar signs, and advertising and photo contests. Magazine advertisements played a starring role in the strategy, setting the tone and driving the other methods. Dealers were responsible for knowing the themes and directions of the national magazine campaigns and for planning their approaches accordingly. The national company provided posters, postcards, streetcar signs, and advertising cuts that local dealers could use in their hometown newspapers. As the first circular noted, "Local news paper advertising is the landing net which scoops up the fish caught on the magazine hooks. The hooks are full, get out your landing net."[9]

Window displays functioned as one local hook. In May 1902, the *Kodak Trade Circular* emphasized the importance of vacations to the photo business and also reiterated the dealer's obligation to strategize according to the calendar: "The time is ripe. Millions of people with vacation money jingling in their pockets will see our Kodak advertising in the next two weeks. This advertising tells them to buy of you. We have awakened their interest. You can cinch the bargain by an irresistible display of Kodaks and Kodak pictures and Kodak signs in your window."[10] The circular offered specific visual instructions on creating an attractive display, such as the 1908 exhibit featuring a suitcase full of photographic supplies in front of a sign declaring, "Put a dark room in your suitcase." A similar strategy aimed at traveling couples appeared in "Three's no crowd when the third's a Kodak," which featured two suitcases, two traveling coats, and between them a Kodak, a sign with the tagline, and a large visual of a woman in her traveling clothes checking her camera.[11] A 1911 *Kodak Trade Circular* story featured a "Take a Kodak with You" display design that outlined the company's exhibition philosophy. In describing a display of four frames, three with enlarged vacation photos and one with a notebook, camera, pencil, and snapshots affixed held together with the tagline "Take a Kodak with you," the story noted that the "show window must be as neat as your best dressed salesman in the store, and being deprived of the power of speech, must present its argument in some novel and striking manner." That approach included limiting the number of items so as not to confuse the viewer, creating a single message that salesmen could build upon when face-to-face with the customer, and putting oneself in the viewer's position to think about what items would be appealing. The instructions even included a sentence to handwrite on the displayed notebook: "Spent the day along the banks of the river. It is most picturesque and winds among beautiful hills, and tall trees stand like sentinels along the bank. Writing cannot describe at all adequately, its real beauty." To emphasize that observation, the display included small- and large-sized photos of the scene described.[12]

Kodak's instructions for displays were not always one-way communications to dealers, though; the company hosted window display contests to gather ideas from dealers and published helpful (and replicable) display instructions from individual dealers. In May 1911 the *Kodak Trade Circular* published instructions on how to re-create a window design by R. S. Miller from the J. C. Coblentz Drug Company in Bloomington, Indiana. The display included a large central sign declaring, "Wherever you go, however you go, take a Kodak with you," superimposed on a large map of the United States. An adjacent sign oriented perpendicularly to the main sign read, "Start out with a Kodak." Different-colored ribbons connected the maps to a model ship, car, plane, and train, and all of them were connected to the Kodak, emphasizing a monumental relationship among space, travel, and its documentation.[13] Kodak encouraged such submissions with window display contests, in which dealers won cash prizes for the best exhibits. Starting in 1897, Kodak also hosted advertising contests, sometimes for newspaper advertising ideas and sometimes for window displays. Such crowdsourcing allowed local dealers to participate in the national advertising process and benefit from prize money. In 1909 Kodak offered dealers prizes ranging from $5 to $100 for window display ideas. The competition was divided into "Class A" windows (eight feet or more in width) and "Class B" windows (less than eight feet in width), and participants could win one of ten cash prizes. The judges came from the advertising industry, "men whose standing will be a guarantee that the prizes will be awarded to those whose displays are the most attractive from an advertising standpoint."[14] Walter Encott, a Kodak dealer from Louisville, Kentucky, and winner of multiple contests, appreciated the opportunity to participate in the national advertising effort and attributed his rising sales directly to advertising through window displays and local newspapers.[15]

Eastman Kodak centralized its advertising at the national level by developing concepts for magazine and newspaper ads, hiring artists, and overseeing the design. Once the magazine ads had been developed, the company created versions for local newspapers and shared them as ad cuts along with directions on placement. Dealers could then choose from the ad cuts, request them from Rochester, and arrange for ad space in local papers. Because Kodak depended on its dealers to maintain a consistent brand message, it provided careful instructions on using the cuts. In a 1903 letter enclosed with cuts, Kodak provided one dealer with the language to be used for communicating with publishers (for example, explaining the difference between halftones and outline and their applications) and reassured the dealer that he was doing the right thing by taking out local newspapers ads: "Results come quickly from local Kodak advertising, because we have prepared the way, because people know Kodaks by reputation. You have only to tell that you have them and about new things."[16] The *Kodak Trade Circular* provided news of new cuts and instructions on using them. In 1912 the circular offered a primer in "The Principles of Advertising," telling dealers to time their ads carefully to their communities' interests and the national advertising schedule, design ads for the reader who won't spend much time looking at the ad ("plan our 'copy' so that 'he who runs may read'"), allow for space on the page, keep sentences brief, avoid "funnyisms" and too many different typefaces, and "always underestimate rather than overestimate your goods."[17] The *Kodak Trade Circular* also kept dealers informed about other types of local advertising such as streetcar signs and postcards. This system allowed Kodak to expand internationally and at the same time maintain control over its brand. Ad cuts, streetcar signs, and post-cards also enabled dealers to reach local consumers with messages that would be consistent from country to city and across national boundaries.

These messages centered on memory and mobility. The Eastman Kodak Company was sensitive to the functions of tourism in American life, and it made travel a central theme of its advertising. In an interview with *Printer's Ink* in 1918, Lewis B. Jones, who had headed Kodak's marketing since 1892, noted that two main reasons existed for purchasing a camera: children and travel.[18] Writing in 1888 to an early potential customer for the Kodak, George Eastman noted: "We think you would be well pleased with the Kodak as a traveling companion on your ocean trip. Some of the first sold were to parties starting upon European trips, and we have from them and other tourists many testimonials of the satisfaction they have had in using the Kodak."[19] An 1890 ad in *World Traveller* declared the Kodak was "essentially a tourist's camera."[20] In the early 1900s, Kodak issued an ad series that appealed to American vacationers' desire to use their leisure time fruitfully; ads urged consumers to "Take a Kodak with you" or asserted more baldly, "A vacation without a Kodak is a vacation wasted." As one ad claimed, "'Vacation' means more if you Kodak." The ads featured a young woman identified in some as the "Kodak Girl" in all her travel finery, carrying a camera and surrounded by images evoking the pleasures of travel: flowing flora, beautiful scenery, and trains heading off to the horizon. One even identified the destination: "Take a Kodak with you to the Pan-American

Exposition." These early touristic camera ads appeared in popular periodicals such as the *Ladies' Home Journal, Youth's Companion, Leslie's Weekly,* and *Saturday Evening Post.* In this early period of mass photography, when both company and consumers used "Kodak" as a verb, Eastman Kodak assured its customers that the Kodak made them smarter consumers because "the Kodaker has all the vacation delights that others have—and has pictures besides."[21]

By 1905, Kodak refined its message about the camera, making the vacation productive by including a sense of the past, a process the historian Nancy Martha West refers to as the making of the photograph as an "instant artifact."[22] Kodak ran an ad in *Outing Magazine* in 1905 with the tagline "Bring your Vacation Home in a Kodak," which featured three smartly dressed vacationers (two with cameras) in Holland taking photographs of a Dutch couple. With an image drawn by the well-known graphic artist Edward Penfield, the ad evoked the past in two ways. First, it visually stressed the distinction between the modern, stylishly dressed tourists and the traditionally dressed Dutch couple, complete with wooden shoes, by setting them at opposite sides of the image. In the background, a silhouette of a windmill divides the two groups. On the right side is modernity, while on the left is tradition. Second, the text identified the present moment as tomorrow's history: "Add to the afterdelights of your holiday with pictures of the people, the places, and the sports you're interested in." The camera, then, was a tool against forgetting, a tool of control that evidenced one's modernity. Kodak's 1905 ad "The Kodak Girl in Fair Japan," featuring an unusual watercolor image created by the accomplished illustrator Charles Allan Gilbert of a young white woman being pulled through a Japanese garden by a rickshaw operator (figure 4), demonstrates contradictory themes about tourism and the past. As Nancy Martha West rightly notes, the relationship between the figures reinforces a presumed superiority of Western culture. The "Kodak Girl" is above the Japanese man; her finery bespeaks beauty and accomplishment, and the whiteness of her skin and clothing evokes the racial hierarchy of early twentieth-century American society. West argues that the "similarity of their expressions, poses, and even facial features forms a stunning focal point for this advertisement, suggesting as it does the confluence of American and Japanese beauty."[23] When viewed in the context of late nineteenth-century ideas about time and progress, however, the message is more about hierarchy than alignment. The similarity of their positions and expressions, paired with the lower

Figure 4. "Kodak Simplicity," Kodak advertisement, 1905, Emergence of Advertising in America, John W. Hartman Center for Sales, Advertising, and Marketing History, Rubenstein Library, Duke University.

position of the Japanese figure engaged in the manual labor of tourist transport, recalls the nineteenth-century stereotype of the Japanese as "imitative" (and therefore inferior) and failed to recognize Japan's rapid industrialization.[24] The ad functioned rhetorically by emphasizing a distinction between the visited (those associated with the past, tradition, and heritage) and the visitors (those wearing the latest fashions and using the latest technology).

The idea of tourism as a marker of middle-class status, modernity, and control over the meanings of history for white women appeared in a number of Kodak advertisements. The 1909 "They All Remembered the Kodak" ad in *Collier's Weekly* worked on consumer anxiety about status by showing a group of travelers with their trunks. At the center of the group, a young woman in a light-colored duster peers into a camera bag while others admire it. The text evokes the same anxieties about purposeful vacations and the passage of time as in other ads: "A vacation *without* a Kodak is a vacation wasted. A Kodak doubles the value of every journey and adds to the pleasure, present and future, of every outing. Take a Kodak with you."[25] Smart dressing, according to the ads, went well with technological mastery and control, a theme fitting the camera neatly into a complex of modern consumer habits and desires.[26] In "There's more to the vacation when you Kodak" from 1908, a fashionably dressed young woman with a broad smile looks directly at the viewer as she clutches a Kodak to her chest. The fullness of her dress indicates an embrace of consumer pleasure and excess, but the text refers to the importance of making the most of one's vacation, presumably because it was a hard-earned occasion.[27] Consumer technologies, in the world of the ads, attested to white female freedoms and competence. One version of "Take a Kodak with you" from *Collier's Weekly* in 1908 depicts a young woman in travel clothes with her foot set squarely—and not at all demurely—on top of her suitcase, which is covered with ten distinct labels affirming her experience as a traveler. Her attention, though, is on her camera, which she is adjusting, an indication of her technological skill. Another young white female traveler appears in a *Saturday Evening Post* ad in 1908 as she—and she alone—walks up to the past in the form of the US Capitol. Smiling at the viewer, who watches her approach the seat of political power, she evokes confidence and purpose. While the tagline "There's twice the pleasure in the journey, and twice the pleasure afterward—if you Kodak" references tourism, the implications of a young woman headed toward the Capitol could not have been lost on *Post* readers in the years immediately preceding the passage of the Nineteenth Amendment to the Constitution, giving women the right to vote.[28]

The combination of temporal awareness and youth appeared in other Kodak marketing. The young, who may not have worried much about the rapid passage of time, had the Eastman Kodak Company to remind them. A 1909 ad in *Youth's Companion* encouraged young people to document their outings in anticipation of future bouts of nostalgia: "There's twice the pleasure in every outing for those who Kodak. Not merely the increased pleasure of the day's trip, but afterward, added pleasure in the possession of pictures of people and places and incidents that have gone to make up the day's enjoyment."[29] Indeed, the passage of time as marked by the growth of children provided a central theme to the series "Let the children Kodak." One 1909 ad published in *Ladies' Home Journal* neatly summarized the dual purpose of the camera in the family with children: "Let the children Kodak. And then in turn Kodak the children. In every home, on every vacation trip, there's a story for the Kodak to record. But above all is the serial story of the children, from the days of wild gallops across the nursery floor upon the fractious rocking-horse to the foot ball days; from the days of tending dollies to graduation days."[30] The certainty of children's development provoked parental anxiety about missing key moments—moments that Kodak offered to record. One ad depicted a family on the front stoop with the son and father posing for a camera held by the mother. The male dyad is decked out in hunting gear—father with a gun and son with a camera—as the mother and grandmother (whose shawl and gray hair underscore the inevitability of change) look on. The text reads: "This is a big day for Ed, Junior. To be allowed to go hunting with dad is a real event—and calls for a picture as a matter of course. Little story-telling incidents like this make the best kind of Kodak pictures. They are happening every day at your house."[31]

Kodak marketing touched on both modernity and its capacity to create unease about the rapidity of change. Mass photography served the busy touristic activity of the growing managerial and professional class of the late nineteenth century by becoming a release (as well as a cause) for some of the tensions inherent in the industrial culture's shifting perceptions of time. As historians of technology demonstrate, timekeeping emerged as a central fascination of the nineteenth century as mechanization shortened the length of time required to complete work and at the same time made synchronization of work—scheduling—more crucial to conducting one's life. The cultural historian Alexis McCrossen notes that a number of nineteenth-century innovations such as "steam engines, gaslight, telegraphs, telephones, electricity, phonography, photography, combustion engines, and wireless communication" altered "social experience of time and space."[32] Mass photography, however, could allow users to feel more in control of time by documenting their own lives for posterity as well as recording the scenes and people they felt would be inevitably changed forever by modernity.

Around 1910 Eastman Kodak's thematic combinations of travel, technological modernity, and anxiety over the passage of time became more aggressive toward the world beyond the company's own consumers and started to take on imperialistic tones, offering a more subtle yet nonetheless resonant message akin to Rudyard Kipling's 1899 call for Americans to "take up the White Man's burden" and "send forth the best ye breed" to guide the uncivilized toward modernity. (Interestingly, Kipling himself had endorsed the Pocket Kodak in an 1896 ad.)[33] In the 1910s and throughout the 1920s, the themes shifted toward stronger impulses of capture. Instead of simply asking tourists to "take a Kodak with you" as they had done earlier, the ads switched the emphasis to the rest of the world, asserting that it needed to have its picture taken: "All outdoors invites your Kodak." This series featured men engaged in outdoor hobbies like canoeing, hunting, or biking; women sailing, stepping from automobiles, sitting in parks, or walking on beaches, and groups of young people enjoying golf or spring blossoms. The shift in perspective was an ideational step toward even bolder ads such as the 1912 "The World is mine" ad discussed at the beginning of this chapter. A 1913 ad in *Country Life in America* bears a visual resemblance to "The World is mine," for the Kodak Girl now appears at the left in the same type of columnar travel suit, her feet in a stance of solidity, aiming her camera at a foreign landscape. The ad instructs the consumer to "let pictures, made from your own point of view, keep the story of your own personal impressions," reinforcing the importance of the consumer's individual perspectives.[34] A 1913 *Life* magazine illustration (reproduced in a trade circular) offered a humorous take on Kodak's assertion that the camera allowed tourists to better shape their own perspectives of the world. Accompanying an image of a well-dressed man and woman pointing a camera at the Leaning Tower of Pisa is a dialogue that reads: "'You're not holding your Kodak level.' 'Yes—but it's the only way I can get the tower straight.'"[35]

Eastman Kodak marketed the idea that modernity brought control over both space and time, sometimes using ads that drew on the cultural symbols of imperialism and white masculinity. The company associated control of space through both tourism and war with the recording of international history as early as 1904 with its ad "In war as in peace The Kodak is at the front." Featuring a reproduction of a Frederic Remington painting depicting a war correspondent standing resolutely in the foreground as a dark figure in white tends horses in the background, the ad claims: "In Cuba and the Philippines, in South Africa, in Venezuela, and now in Korea and Manchuria, the camera more in evidence is the Kodak. The same qualities that make it indispensable to the correspondent make it more desirable for the tourist—simplicity, freedom from darkroom, lightness combined with a strength that resists the wear and tear of travel."[36] In 1913 the *Saturday Evening Post* carried a Kodak ad that evoked the white American man outdoors as a symbol of mastery over nature and people considered "primitive."[37] Featuring a photographic image of a young man firmly holding a Kodak, chin held high, looking outward over the wild landscape as a glow from the sky shines directly behind the subject, the ad claims: "Every photographic need for every outing is anticipated in the Kodak. Surveyor, hunter, tourist, explorer—all those whose business takes them out into the open, or who find their pleasure there, have proved its useful companionship."[38] A similar ad published in *Collier's Weekly* in 1909 depicts a man carrying full camping gear on his back poised on one knee, framing a photograph; the ad declares, "There are no game laws for those who hunt with a Kodak."[39] As the historian Finis Dunaway has found, for privileged men of the late nineteenth century, the camera represented a higher form of the hunt. In this dynamic, the camera operated as a tool of memory similar to taxidermy.[40] That Kodak's list of "manly" activities—"surveyor, hunter, tourist, explorer"—included tourism in this context is not surprising, for despite its associations with European hotels and high-end steamships, tourism could be fashioned as masculine control over images of "premodern" peoples, animals, and outdoor spaces.

In the interwar years, Kodak introduced motion pictures as a way to extend the power of the camera. In a 1919 ad promoting its new motion picture technology, Kodak claimed that, thanks to its efforts in global market expansion and its support for tourists, "one-half the world now knows how the other half lives." The ad also assured American consumers of their cultural and technological superiority in the equation:

"You sit in a comfortable auditorium, watching the Zulu in his native dance, while out in the Dark Continent the savage sees the Easter parade on Fifth Avenue."[41] The ad depicts the earth floating against a light background, the United States centralized in the planet's orientation, as a strip of film featuring images of landmarks from around the world loops downward from the North Pole. In the foreground, a muscled, spear-wielding "Zulu" stands at ease while watching an image of the New York City Easter Parade on a screen that bisects the global filmstrip. The ad evoked the class distinction between the gazers and the gazed upon established by Jacob Riis's 1890 photographic window into American urban poverty, *How the Other Half Lives*, while also declaring that the world had become smaller and more knowable through photography. In this way it captured the early twentieth-century relationships among photography, tourism, class privilege, and Americans' expanded ideas about their roles in global affairs. Less subtle visually, but paired significantly with the spatial assessment of modernity, was the statement of a temporal theme: "Photography today is a part of life. It touches every human interest, holds fast the memories of the home, is the right hand of science, the scout in war and truthful chronicler of history." Thus Eastman's innovation not only ordered the world into two unequal halves, each one knowing the other through images, but also tasked its users with producing tomorrow's history by recording today's world. While the "halves" of the world knew each other through the recorded image, the "haves" of the world were charged with recording for posterity, an idea advanced to sell cameras—and one that relied on the growth of both mass tourism and modern advertising.

Chapter Three

"SIDE TRIPS IN CAMERA-LAND"
Tourism and the Visual Record

In 1915, writing in *Photo Era Magazine,* William Ludlum referred to his trip to "one of the little towns on the mosquito shore of Long Island" as one of his "Side Trips in Camera-Land." To him, the place itself was secondary to the opportunity it provided to capture it through the lens; it was a land for making photographs. Ludlum framed Camera-Land in terms of a hunting outing or safari, only instead of a gun, he took a camera: "I wear my little 'black box' . . . as I do my hat or shoes. I don't always make use of it, but I bear in mind 'the things that happen when you haven't got a gun' and carry a supply of photographic ammunition for such emergencies."[1] Other commenters on tourist photography spoke to the broadening practice of touring what Ludlum called "Camera-Land." An anonymous author writing in *The Outlook* in 1909 made fun of women's professed antipathy toward taking photos while on vacation. The author had overheard a young woman talking about her vacation plans for Europe, which included a pledge *"not* [to] commit the vulgarity of snapping my camera in the faces of foreign peasants as if they were part of the scenery. I think it's indecent!" The author found this amusing, for his wife had professed the same thing before she took up the camera, but her transformation had been quick: "Marvelous indeed is it to watch in the most sensitive of the gentler sex the development of what might be termed the photographic nerve." It took only one week with a camera on tour before his wife was keeping "photographically 'covered' some moving victim, some 'perfectly delicious fishwife,' or some grandam striding homeward with half a dozen butter-tubs in a pannier upon her back."[2] The first generation of mass portable photographers worked to naturalize the practice through a diversity of concepts: the camera as a gun, as a marker of modernity, as a method of meeting one's responsibility to record history, and as a tool to help assert one's existence. Camera users gave meaning to photography according to the ways in which positionality informed the user's mobility and relationship to public spaces. This went far beyond the instructions provided by Kodak marketing, as camerists worked out their own ideas of personal visual legacy, sometimes replicating the privilege assumed by Kodak ads, but at other times pushing explicitly and implicitly against the conventions and violence of white supremacy and elitism inherent in tourist infrastructure and public space.

Some tourist photographers developed a style and an aesthetic that combined popular artistic and professional uses of photography with the imperatives of the upper-middle-class vacation. Nowhere was this more apparent than in tourists' approaches to photographing architecture and ruins, which drew on conventions of record photography and picturesque landscape painting. As the visual historian Elizabeth Edwards has shown, photography provided an outlet for shaping understandings of the past. Record photography—in which professionals and amateurs alike set out to record the features and settings of historic buildings—promoted the idea that modernity put the bucolic agrarian past in danger. The modern technology of the camera could be used to record historic buildings and, according to the popular ethnographic literature of the day, the peoples who had survived modern life.[3] While a romantic anti-modernism informed record and ethnographic photography, both styles drew on the emerging social sciences for support and method. Another tradition informing tourism photography was that of the picturesque, which had been firmly established in America in the early nineteenth century as a visual tradition associated with tourism. American writers and artists took cues from their colleagues in Europe and started to rethink wild places. Instead of places to fear, natural landscapes could be sources of inspiration. This idea appealed to Americans—who had fewer ruins at hand than Europeans—and, as the art historian Richard Gassan notes, became the basis for the Hudson River School of painting. Painters rendered detailed, dramatic, and romantic landscapes, offering viewers an emotional connection with wild places. Tourists all over America from the Hudson River to Yellowstone framed their photographic scenes for full drama in the tradition of the picturesque landscape.[4]

Tourist photo albums consistently combined a focus on the past with a focus on the picturesque, even if they reflected different classed and gendered styles of display. Wealthier album creators tended to hire professional photographers and bookbinders to make presentation pieces for fellow travelers and business associates, while travelers of more modest means took the do-it-yourself approach to both presentation albums and souvenir albums. An album attributed to the wealthy Western Union heir James Sibley Watson Sr. documenting a hunting trip taken to the western United States in 1885 reflected the tendency of the wealthy to create large gilded albums with one single oversize print per page. Including images of scenery, camp scenes, and the hunters' kills, the album offered evidence of Watson and his male companions "roughing it" in a place they viewed as untouched by the technological modernity this New York businessman had helped to bring about.[5] The wife of Dr. Spencer Franklin produced a different kind of album for a 1903–4 trip to Mexico, Cuba, and Puerto Rico: four folios that were more colloquial and personal. Mrs. Franklin took great care in arranging the photos herself and providing captions for almost every one, adding comments on methods of travel, sites visited, the tourists' states of mind, and various references to time, such as describing things as "old," "antiquities," or of the "present." She consistently labeled photos of Dr. Franklin "my hubby." Unlike James Watson's large presentation album, Mrs. Franklin's album contained many small snapshots of views, locals, and tourists, each with its handwritten caption. She created an intimate memory book, probably meant as a centerpiece for discussion with close family and friends.[6]

Whether wealthy travelers creating formal presentation albums or middle-class adventurers putting together collections of snapshots, American tourists took a particular liking to Europe and the built and ruined environments that Mark Twain saw as "dust and decay." France and Italy in particular offered Americans the visual evidence of the past and a way into the sublime mystery of premodern life which they sought desperately in landscape tourism at home. In 1916, writing in *Photo Era*, Herbert Turner summed up Americans' attraction to the French countryside as an escape: "We, as Americans, can little realize—in these modern times of complicated existence, of electric wonders, of skyscrapers, and of hurry and bustle—that in France there yet exist mediaeval towns whose inhabitants live the same life, for the most part, as centuries ago and that the external appearance of these towns has changed but little." Turner aimed his camera particularly at Carcassonne, which looked "like a picture in some book of fairy tales." Instead of reading the book, though, Turner reframed the landscape as a theatrical event for tourist eyes: "Imagine a dream-castle that contains, within, a goodly city of crooked streets lined with picturesque old houses, a delightful church of the eleventh century with some exquisite stained-glass windows, and a chateau, the like of which, for sheer theatrical mediaevalism of form, one can hardly match in Western Europe."[7]

When Godfrey Priester found himself "With a Camera in Italy" in 1927, he revealed the power of historical landscapes for spiritual inspiration, for among the ruins, "one's imagination rises to a higher plane" as the surroundings remind the traveler of "Greek Mythology, Classical Rome, the Crusades, the Renaissance, Mythology and History, Art and Literature," all of which have "left imperishable imprints on this beautiful spot of the old world." Often, tourist photographers marveled at the survival abilities of European buildings, another feature of their inherent mystery. Even if its survival was incomplete, the building's remains could be appreciated by tourist photographers; Priester noted that the drama in the environment was ideal for picture taking, for even "in their withered state," the ruins' "artistic lines and perfect proportions compel the admiration of the beholder."[8]

When American tourists turned their cameras on their own country, they sought something that looked different from what they experienced in their non-vacationing lives. Thomas Carpenter, who took his camera on a trip to Florida in 1921 capturing shots of historic buildings, local people, and lots of Spanish moss, urged tourist photographers to look for the unusual, for "if a Florida scene might just as well have been photographed in Massachusetts, why go to Florida after it?"[9] Tourists often chose to photograph people who fit the tourist's image of them, such as Asahel Shurtleff's photo of a "Mexican Indian in Tijuana" pasted in his scrapbook of a trip from Boston to the American West in 1902.[10] For camerist Phil Riley, the United States was something of a consolation prize for the tourist-photographer. He wrote in 1922 that "fortunate indeed is every camerist who is able to travel abroad, extending his knowledge, broadening his vision and increasing his collection of photographs"; but when stuck at home, photographers "are obliged to content ourselves with 'seeing America first,' last, and all the time." Domestic tourists should take heart, though, from landscapes comparable to the finest in the world, for "who indeed can honestly say that Glacier National Park lacks anything of the picturesqueness and grandeur of the best in Switzerland?" Riley noted that the Rocky Mountains had no match in Europe, and that "in the Middle West . . . lie thousands of square miles of plains, prairies, and desert lands as fascinating as the steppes of Russia, the veldt of Africa and the wastes of Arabia."[11]

In contrast to accounts of travel in Europe, records of travels in the United States connected vacation photography with automobility. Unlike the guided tour, the automobile tour provided to most drivers the flexibility to stop and compose shots whenever and wherever the camerist wanted. Frank Reeves, who traveled by car from central Texas to Los Angeles and then on to Yellowstone in 1928 noted that "for those that enjoy photographing, automobile touring is in a class by itself. You not only have your own means to get around, but you can stop when and where you choose and stay as long as you wish—quite an advantage over the regular sight-seeing tours that move on a set schedule."[12] Instead of fixing his camera on castles and cathedrals, Reeves discovered scenic roadways (his photos often included the road itself), pueblos, and people.

Americans touring Egypt found imperial power to be rather glamorous, and climbing on ruins injected adventure into an otherwise posh vacation in hotels built for the British. In 1928 W. Robert Moore captioned his photograph of tourists on camels in front of the Sphinx "the World's Most Famous Studio," referring to the British tradition of having one's photo taken at the spot. Americans followed.[13] Nineteen-year-old Louisa Stephens Wright in 1891 described a rigorous trip to the Sphinx and the pyramids that resulted in a flash-lit Kodak of tourists perched on a sarcophagus. The young traveler was less impressed with the antiquities than she was with the British guests at her hotel: "The crowd at dinner was a gaily robed and attractive one. Evening gowns, very décolleté, many jewels. Men in dinner jackets. . . . O! I am so happy!" This was a significantly different description from the one she applied to her Egyptian hosts, whom she called a "perfect mob."[14]

Louisa Wright's interaction with both the built environment and the people she met on her trip to Egypt reflected the idea that one's relationship to the past indicated one's status in the present. When more privileged American tourists photographed other people, they did so because they considered them both quaint and different from themselves. For these tourists, the camera became both a tool of power and a prop denoting modernity. Amateur camerists on tour took cues from professional ethnographic photographers in popular publications like *National Geographic*. Maynard Owen Williams, writing in *National Geographic* in an essay titled "Adventures with a Camera in Many Lands," claimed that "the snap-shot photograph . . . satisfies man's desire to extend his horizon, to reach out into the unknown, and to identify himself a little more closely with the world of which he is a part." Despite his assertion that "the photograph is a basis for friendly understanding," he spent a great deal of time sneaking shots, bribing subjects, and stalking people in the name of a good photograph. Indeed, he likened snapshot photography abroad to hunting: "No hunter can boast of so satisfactory a bag as falls to him who hunts with the clairvoyant eye of the camera. The focusing knob of the graflex is a more thrilling bit of mechanism than the trigger of a rifle." Williams offered advice to other traveler-photographers such as not to pay subjects, for "one can be given privileges that he cannot buy." With an empty metal film canister, he won the "privilege" of snapping one child who cried, asking not to have her photo taken. Her father, however, had "feared that if his daughter balked he might be subjected to censure," because Williams had a private railcar and therefore must be a man of importance. One woman, who seemed to indicate permission to be photographed, asked through an interpreter not to have the photo sent to her, for she would risk violence from her husband if he knew she had allowed her image to be taken.[15] Some touring camerists were completely surprised by their subjects' desire for privacy and interpreted their hesitancy as a lack of understanding of the modern world.

Tourist photographers noted that the novelty of the camera in distant lands often gave them an in for getting permission to take a shot as well as evidenced the superstitions of those they visited. As a caption for a photograph of a Buddhist monk inspecting a camera, Williams wrote, "At first [the monks] resented being photographed, but after looking through the camera themselves they were delighted to pose for the camera man."[16] On a trip through the American West in 1891, Fannie Miller reported to her diary an exchange her husband had with a mother who emerged from "a wretched looking dwelling" and insisted on having her child's "picter" taken. Her husband "kodaked the little Mormon," who forgot to give him her address, "so the doting mother will long wait of the 'picter' of her darling, that can never come."[17] Frank Reeves hinted at his interactions with the "locals" in New Mexico when he observed that some "superstitions" might emerge from resentment at being photographed: "Some Indians hesitate to have their pictures made through superstition, but most desire to be paid. You can't blame them for this; I can't say that I would take very kindly to the idea of posing for a stranger to make my picture for his pleasure—especially if he ordered me around in the manner some employ when talking to Indians."[18] Williams also revealed that this resistance had less to do with superstition than with resentment of class privilege: "The people . . . are suspicious of those camera hunters who stalk their game from the cushions of an automobile."[19]

The behavior of some touring camerists became so notorious that by the spring of 1925, *Photo Era* used its editorial to provide etiquette training for the "average American tourist," who, "justly or otherwise, has earned a reputation for deportment that is less than flattering." He reminded travelers to say "thank you" when appropriate, avoid displaying the American flag in hotel or lapel, and respect signs that say "Verboten," "Défendu," or "Prohibito."[20] Gertrude Levy wrote that "camera-enthusiasts do no sight-seeing in Europe—they merely search for places to make pictures," a habit sure to make the photographer "regarded with suspicion by friends."[21] There is ample evidence of such misbehavior. W. Robert Moore was so intent on getting a good shot at the waterfront in Panama that he upended a coal cart, which brought "a constant stream of inelegant Spanish" from the woman using the cart.[22] The anonymous writer in *The Outlook* relished the development of his wife's "photographic nerve" so much that he related with enthusiasm the chaos she caused on her trip: "She didn't mind being conspicuous, nor trespassing on private property, nor breaking the laws of Norway, provided a picture was to be had." Her "crowning" photographic achievement—a photo of a "grotesque little wooden figurehead over the door of an ancient Hanseatic fish-gaarde"—was also evidence of her transformation from delicate lady to tourist photographer. He found his "retiring, formerly law-abiding little wife mounted firmly upon a great fish-truck which she had somehow managed to drag across the trolley-line, unconcernedly holding up the passenger traffic of Bergen. A blue-coated official was making agitated representations to her ... but not till the click of a button told of victory won was that intrepid photographer induced to descend."[23] In his estimations, lack of consideration for others was a requirement of tourist photography.

Obnoxious behavior was so much a part of both public and private dialogue about tourist photography that an account characterized exclusively by awe and respect stood out as exceptional. Forty-one-year-old Katherine Fiske Berry's 1919 trip to Japan was notable for the relationship between her, the culture of her hosts, and the camera; she seemed to recognize she was a guest and that the heritage of her hosts was theirs, not hers to use for her own amusement. Writing to her father of a visit to the home of his Japanese associate, a Mr. Ito, she wrote: "Could I have fainted to express my amazement and gratitude, or something more dramatic than a low bow of humility, at such grandeur thrust on me! ME! ME! Gee, whiz, gosh!—not a very elegant expression, but expressive." Mr. Ito arranged for photographs to be taken for her in his garden, and she was drawn to an old bonsai tree for its connection to the past: "The tree pot was carried to a good place and photographed! Imagine my feelings!—We wandered about the rows, and he talked about them as if they were almost human. When you stop to think of it, you can imagine about the people who lived their lives beside these little trees, and passed on, to be replaced by others who cared for and watered them. Think of it, three or four times a day for those hundreds of years!"[24] When she asked if she could photograph his garden, he brought out a photographer hired for the purpose. When she expressed interest in wanting to take her own shots, she arranged to go back later to make her personal mementos.

Personal travel albums produced by the very wealthy often conveyed a sense of ownership over the places pictured. The souvenir album owned by J. George Kaelber of Rochester, New York, documenting a trip to the western United States represents a top-of-the-line tourist album. In 1907 George F. Roth, president of the Rochester Carting Company (a freight-handling operation), treated a small party of his friends and their wives to a western journey with him, about seven thousand miles total, from Rochester to the West Coast in a private train car named "J'arilla." Either the party included a professional photographer or one of the tourists knew photography well, for the resulting album features highly crafted, carefully managed shots, including landscapes and a street scene, but mostly group shots. The album, presented to "Die Genossenschaft" ("the cooperative," members of the touring party) and engraved with individuals' names, included more than photos; it also contained a detailed log, itineraries, letters, and reproductions of news clippings that covered the excursion, such as "Men of Millions View Rose City: Jolly Party from Rochester Making Pleasure Tour of Pacific Coast," "Eastern Capital for Salt Lake: Man Who Installed First Electric Light System Here Marvels at Growth of City," "Party of Rochesterians Feted by Governor of Idaho," and, most simply, "Capitalists from East Here." Each page contains only one photo, professionally matted and captioned. Most show the group, posed as such, on a terrace at their hotel, on a large rock in a lake, or near their cars or railcars. Many make the group the central topic of the image, but in group shots with a car or railcar, the mode of transportation takes center stage. The captions are brief, naming the place where the photo was taken, often referencing the special receptions or entertainments the party enjoyed. When they visited California, they posed with giant trees. In one, they are posed on a massive fallen tree, and the caption reads, "Taking Possession of 'Old Monarch.' Mariposa Park." This reflected one of the album's main themes: no stunning vista or tourist attraction could match the importance of the group itself. Two shots of Yosemite scenes evoke awe, but for the most part, the album privileges the party over the place.[25]

Turn-of-the-century society gave captains of industry few opportunities to experience marginalization, and the album shows that this set felt a responsibility for recording history, meaning their actions as leaders of progress in the United States. They showed an awareness of their future roles in history by designating one of their set a "historian," an act common to club culture at the time. In the early 1900s, the Rochester city directory listed George Roth as a member of the Automobile Club, the Masonic Club, the Rochester Club (of which he was vice president in 1903), the Athletic Club, and the Monroe Club.[26] The group followed several protocols of clubs, designating officers, giving themselves a name, employing their own slang, so the designation of John George Kaelber as historian is consistent with the group dynamic. In 1907 Kaelber was a forty-seven-year-old manager who had emigrated from Germany in 1873. His wife, Matilda, like Roth, was born to German parents, providing the Kaelbers and the Roths ethnic as well as professional and social ties.[27] Other than Roth, Kaelber is one of the few who appear alone; a photo of him with a small ostrich is captioned "Our historian fondling an ostrich, two days old, Ostrich Farm, Pasadena." The trip and the construction of its memory gave Kaelber and his fellow travelers an opportunity to ingratiate themselves with a wealthier, very well-connected company president, and they took the opportunity seriously, highlighting Roth's central role in organizing the trip. The frontispiece of the album reads, "In remembrance of their glorious trip to the western country, enjoyed through the courtesy of Mr. and Mrs. George F. Roth, this souvenir is dedicated by the 'Manager' to his fellow travelers of 'Die Genossenschaft.'" On the same page as the dedication, Kaelber included a head-and-shoulders portrait of Roth.[28] In the album, the centrality of Roth and his party over the places visited reveals the trip to have been more about Rochester society and its professional opportunities than about "discovering" the West. Historical memory via the photograph album cemented social and professional ties.

While the Roth party used the American West as a stage to set their own drama of social position, the 1900–1901 album created by W. S. Wheeler demonstrated marked differences in photo documentation from place to place. The Wheeler party, consisting of two men and two women, toured Europe, the Near East, and Egypt. They documented Europe's impressive architectural sites and ruins with an emphasis on the picturesque. Their European photos included none of themselves, but when they got to Egypt, they pictured themselves often. They posed with their guides and with one another. In some shots they are riding donkeys and camels, while in others they stand dressed in their finery, their elbows resting casually on the structures about them. They hold their chins high. They climb on ruins, even getting into a sarcophagus to imitate the pose of a mummy. One image shows the two men of the party holding umbrellas as a shield from the sun, one of them smoking a cigarette, sitting in sarcophagi as if they were in bathtubs (figure 5). While they did not photograph children in Europe, they did train their cameras on Egyptian children, especially if they were naked or wearing tattered clothing. The resulting images showed children lined up to pose but not looking happy or at all comfortable with having their photos taken. Their approach to photography in Egypt placed the travelers at the center of the narrative, while the shots taken in Europe featured the sites themselves.

In 1903 and 1904, Grace Franklin of Manhattan went on the journey of a lifetime. With two other couples, her physician husband, Spencer, and probably their son Richard, around age nine at the time, she traveled throughout Mexico.[29] They visited ruins, toured famous historical

Figure 5. The Wheeler party in Egypt. Snapshot views of Europe, Japan, and Egypt, Eastman Museum Medium Albums Collection, 77: 0508: 1–227. Courtesy of the George Eastman Museum.

buildings, went on camping outings on horseback, tried their hand at shopping in the marketplaces, ate meals that looked like fine dining but also sat on the ground to eat watermelon, and bought artifacts for souvenirs. They even saw the "mummies of Guanajuato," a collection of corpses buried in the 1830s, disinterred in the 1860s and 1870s, and promoted as a tourist attraction by the late nineteenth century.[30] Mrs. Franklin enjoyed visiting ruins, particularly Chichen Itza and Mitla, and made consistent note of the past meeting the present on her trip, whether through the preservation of ruins and historic buildings or through intangible heritage practices like dance. Her family and party took pictures throughout, and when she returned home, she produced a four-folio album about the experience, with photos arranged thematically and meticulously captioned. It was an intimate memory book, in which she referred often to "my hubby" and documented her travel party as well as the landscape, people, and art of Mexico. Her enthusiasm for the trip comes through clearly in both her photos and the attention she paid to arranging and captioning them. The album also shows that she was familiar with the conventions of photography: close-up portraits, domestic snapshots, bird's-eye views, record photography, and even ethnographic typology. While Grace Franklin's album may have been exceptional in quality, it was similar to other albums in the approach it took to personal archiving: the album as a way to put oneself at the center of the narrative.

The Franklins and their party definitely did not rest much. They fished, dined, camped, explored, interacted with the Mexican people, and took photos. The folios include documentation of a bullfight, the eruption of Mount Colima, and rides on boats, in cars, and on burros. Many of the photos show their party laughing and smiling, and such enthusiasm extended to the captions, where Grace Franklin quoted their guides, provided specific place-names, presented historical or anthropological information, commented on architectural features, and offered insight into the feelings of the photo subjects. In their enthusiasm for the trip, the Franklins did not question the order of the social arrangements, however. When the captions quoted their guides, it was often to make fun of their English, such as the caption for a photo of ruins in Mitla, described as: "Another pretty bit. 'They builded better than they knew!'" When captioning a photo of a dance troupe, she noted that the performance was "one old Aztec dance, given for our special benefit." The visitors leaned casually on or climbed elements of the ruins, centering themselves in the photos for both scale and a sense of entitlement. One photo shows Mrs. Franklin and her friend in a white dress with a woman between them engaged in weaving (figure 6). The weaver is barefoot, standing while balancing the loom, engaged in her work; the two tourists stand on either side, not getting too close. The caption reveals that only two of the three women were in on the fun: "Native woman weaving cloth. Indignant because we took her picture." One folio begins with a montage labeled "Types of Mexican People," while another features a photo of a young woman captioned "A Yucatan Belle Native Mestiza dress. Their wealth consists in the amount and quality of embroidery. Also in their rosary." The next photo shows a male member of the touring party flirting with the young woman captioned, "As usual, Friend Tibbal's at it again!" These images and captions demonstrate

My last touch of Mitla

Native woman wearing cloth. Indignant because [we] took her picture.

Only Ruoby lacking from the party

A couple of Mitla friends

Figure 6. Detail from a page of the Franklins' album documenting their trip to Mexico in 1903–4. Courtesy of the George Eastman Museum.

the Franklins' sense of Mexico as a "Camera-Land," an opportunity to center themselves in a place to which they have no claim through birth, descent, culture, language, or nationality.

The Roth, Wheeler, and Franklin albums reveal differences in sensibilities about public space. While the Roth party album showed little of what the West looked like in 1907, it revealed much about the party's desire to be viewed as in control over space and their own narrative. The Wheelers and the Franklins produced albums that recorded the people and places they visited, indicating that they saw themselves as having an instructional role for friends and family who would look at the album. Even in that geography teacher role, however, they presented place in terms of the opportunity it afforded to be arranged and understood by the camera operator. These approaches also reflected class position, for wealth allowed one both to have private space and at the same time to claim authority over public spaces.

Like the "indignant" subject in the Franklin photo whose work was interrupted by white travelers with a camera, the less privileged negotiated camera culture as both photographic subjects and camera users. During the period of growth for portable photography, Native people responded to forced relocations, major land losses, federal and state incursions into their sovereignty, and increasing white violence. As the infrastructure to support eastern white tourism increased in the West, Native people increasingly became the subjects of tourist cameras. The Eastman Kodak Company used this phenomenon in its marketing. One advertising cut for the Kodak Bull's-Eye, Bullet, and Pocket Kodak shared with dealers in the 1890s features six Native people posed in front of a woodpile in dress regalia. The ad must have assumed that readers would relate to such an image, for it failed to mention the subject in the caption. Instead it referenced the camera: "Made with the Bulls-Eye."[31] In 1909, Kodak sponsored the publication of Frederick Monson's booklet "With a Kodak in the Land of the Navajo," instructing dealers that it would provide a model of travel photography for their "high class trade" customers.[32] One exceptionally interesting Kodak advertisement revealed a bit more about Native people's actual responses to tourist photography. Published in the *Kodak Trade Circular* in August 1913, the ad includes a drawing with the familiar tagline "Take a Kodak with you." The illustration features the stylishly dressed Kodak Girl operating a telescoping Pocket Kodak from the steps of a train. Her camera is focused on a Native man holding multiple baskets, wrapped in a woven blanket and wearing a wide-brimmed hat over his chin-length dark hair. The scene was a common one in the early twentieth century, when many tourists in the West stayed close to trains and train stations. Native businesspeople often met the trains to sell tourists art, clothing, and entertainment and to pose for their cameras. The historian Carol J. Williams, in her study of photography in the Pacific Northwest, emphasizes that Native people saw such exchanges in economic terms, despite tourists' sense of entitlement when it came to images of them. She provides a helpful interpretation of Native people's reticence to pose for photos: "Objection to photography was not so much about fear of the camera, or its theft of the soul or spirit of the sitter, as about a growing recognition that pho-

Figure 7. Interrupting the transaction. Native performers using a mirror
to interfere with the camera. Photo by R. R. Whiting, Library of Congress,
Prints & Photographs Division, LC-DIG-stereo-1s03832.

tography constituted another intrusion by the Euro-American that had
to be effectively controlled by the individual. Tourists or travelers initiated a trading negotiation by pointing their camera lens toward the
body, territory, housing, or other proprietary objects. . . . The conception
of the photographic encounter as a form of trade was an enterprising
and innovative strategy on the part of the Native American subject."[33]
The "Take a Kodak with you" ad showing the Kodak Girl taking a photo
of the Native man reveals him as a person navigating multiple transactions. While the Kodak Girl's camera is pointed toward him, he looks
back at the viewer of the ad with an expression of forbearance. His chin
is high and his gaze is directed pointedly at the viewer as if assessing the
simultaneous transactions initiated by both the tourist photographer
and the viewer of the ad.

The central Native figure in the "Take a Kodak with you" train-side
ad demonstrates one response among many shaped by individual personalities as well as different Native cultures, regions, and economies.
In 1904, Richard Ross Whiting of the Whiting View Company of Cincinnati produced a series of stereographs of the Louisiana Purchase
Exposition held in St. Louis. Among the scenes taken of the fair, he sold
two depicting Native people: one a posed group shot of six figures and

two horses, and the other of the same people lined up on horseback (figure 7). The person closest to the photographer shields his face from the camera, while the next-closest person holds a mirror that reflects sunlight into the camera's lens. Whiting's caption explains the strategy of interrupting the transaction: "Indians on Pike at World's Fair trying to prevent picture being made by reflecting sunlight from small mirrors into camera."[34] While it is difficult to know exactly what happened in between the posed shot and the interrupted transaction (perhaps a lack of satisfaction with remuneration if the mirror photo was taken after the posed photo, or a negotiation of terms if the posed photo came later), but what is clear is that these performers maintained some control over their images, which they knew to be salable. Traveler Marian Peabody reported resistance to the tourist lens in western Canada in 1901. She described an incident in which she "descended to being that hateful thing, a cheeky Kodak fiend," when she continued to take photos of "picturesque . . . Indians" even when they indicated they did not want to be the subject of her vacation photos: "I pointed my Kodak at them but they immediately stopped and seemed to hold a pow-wow. I turned away and they came on again and when they were near enough I turned and snapped them. My! They were mad, and I was quite afraid of them but I snapped them again. I thought they would shoot me but they contented themselves with sticking out their tongues and making faces."[35] Carol J. Williams documented multiple occasions when tourists became angry with Native people for insisting on compensation for their images.[36] Martha Sandwiess likewise documented a diversity of Native terms and concepts referring to photography—including the Haida term for the camera which translates as "copying people" and the Makah term for the photograph as "finished design"—indicating the "group-specific nature of early responses to the medium."[37] Whether choosing to pose for a price, behaving in ways that confronted white tourists' stereotypes, or preventing tourists from taking photographs, Native people exercised, in Hulleah Tsinhnahjinnie's term, "photographic sovereignty," the ability to maintain control over one's image and use visual media for self-actualization and self-determination.[38]

Native professional photographers ran successful studios throughout the late nineteenth and early twentieth centuries and modeled photographic behaviors for others in their communities. These photographers employed the power of the image to aid the creation of self-affirming community identities. The Tsimshian scholar Mique'l Askren Dangeli has shown that the work of Benjamin A. Haldane (Tsimshian; 1874–1941), a prolific photographer based in Metlakatla, Alaska, testifies to the use of camera technology for community affirmation and recovery from disruption. Haldane moved with his family (and about eight hundred others) to Metlakatla from British Columbia when he was thirteen years old. In 1899 he set up a photography studio, where he took and processed photos of groups, families, buildings, and landscapes.[39] As Dangeli found, Haldane also documented cultural autonomy: "One of the most significant aspects of B. A. [Haldane]'s work was his participation in, and photographs of potlaches on the Nass River, which at the time were outlawed by the Canadian government. Using his photography as a means of resistance against . . . intrusion on this ceremony in his own community, [Haldane] also took photographs in Metlakatla that made explicit visual references to people's clan lineages and hereditary positions."[40] Dangeli's analysis of Haldane's photographs is particularly important in countering the image promoted by the missionary William Duncan of the Tsimshian as "assimilated."[41]

Like Benjamin Haldane, Richard Throssel, a photographer of Cree, Métis, Scottish, and English ancestry, documented prohibited religious practices that had to be conducted away from white authorities. Throssel was a commercial photographer focused on the Crow Reservation in Montana (he was adopted as Crow in 1905), where he ran the Throssel Photocraft Company.[42] Of the thousands of photos he took of community life, most of them were designed for the non-Native market: portraits in ceremonial clothing, romanticized hunting scenes, dances, and tipis. But unlike many of his white contemporaries photographing Native people, Throssel took numerous pictures that emphasized the individuality of his subjects, using their names in his titles or taking candid shots of family moments. He also respectfully captured a sense of play, such as the shot of a young man's legs sticking up from the river and one of two people sharing a laugh.[43] Horace Poolaw, a Kiowa photographer born in 1906, never operated a studio like Throssel but instead developed his photos in his home. He gained notice for his family portraits, theatrical portraits, depictions of veterans and the military, and images that presented Kiowa in cars, leading scholars to associate him with modern subjects, in distinction to the glass plate–era conventions of Haldane and the staged, Edward Curtis–style subjects of Throssel. (I would point out, however, that Throssel's later work included many modern subjects such as cars, air shows, and motorcycle races.)[44] Amy Lonetree's work on Ho-Chunk uses of photography demonstrates the active roles Native people played in employing family photographs to honor family ties as an act of "survivance." She employs Gerald Vizenor's term to describe Ho-Chunk "strength and perseverance that it took for our people to remain intact as a tribal nation in the aftermath of colonial violence and oppression." Her study of Ho-Chunk portraits taken by the white studio photographer Charles Van Schaick in the years following a series of forced removals and during waves of deadly influenza reveals "images [that] embody the strength and survivance of the Ho-Chunk people and reflect a heritage of resilience."[45]

As scholars of Native photography have noted, snapshot collections by Native people have most often been preserved by families, not public archives.[46] Collections that have been given to public archives speak to experiences of both mobility and commitment to the practice of visual memory. To be sure, extant photo collections do not document the type of tourism typical of wealthy white eastern leisure tourists, whose trips attested to their abilities to afford time away from work and home. Instead, Native snapshots document travel for work or education. Parker McKenzie (Kiowa) is a case in point. Known later for his work in Kiowa linguistics, McKenzie enrolled in the Rainy Mountain Boarding School in Oklahoma in 1904 and continued his education there until 1914, when he moved to the Phoenix Indian Boarding School. Boarding schools were brutal for young Native people, who faced not just separation from families but abuse, hard work, cruel living conditions, and a program of cultural separation meant to assimilate them. Boarding schools, as historians have argued, possessed significant markers of genocide.[47] By no stretch of the imagination could being forced to go to boarding school be termed a vacation, but it was a departure from home. Despite the difficulties, as Nicole Strathman's work has shown, student photographs like McKenzie's depicted moments of leisure away from the rigors of schoolwork when students enjoyed one another's company: playing baseball, talking, going to the movies, and courting.[48] McKenzie produced over three hundred photos of himself and his peers, and while the intent of the boarding schools was to disrupt familial—and hence cultural—ties, such images served an important function in communicating the students' experiences to those at home. McKenzie, the young emerging linguist, sat for his snapshot at the Phoenix School with his typewriter. Staging the photo required moving a desk, chair, and typewriter outdoors, which speaks to McKenzie's intention to communicate his thoughts on his own identity as a writer, a cultural innovator.

Jennie Ross Cobb (Aniyunwiya) took up photography as a child, and her student snapshots at the Cherokee Female Seminary in Tahlequah, Oklahoma, reveal her fascination with community and movement, particularly that of women. As Hulleah Tsinhnahjinne notes, Cobb's snapshots "truly imagined Native women with love."[49] Cobb pictured diverse subjects, including buildings, groups, a historic house, children, and students. She also pictured women paused from motion. Her 1902 "When the Train Came to Tahlequah" centers two women lifting their skirts to walk on newly laid train tracks, the richness of the fabric contrasting with the rough surfaces of the railroad ties. Her camera, unlike those of tourists, elicited smiles from her subjects.[50] Unlike McKenzie, Cobb later went on to work professionally as a photographer, although few of her photos made their way into public archives.[51]

McKenzie and Cobb were not the only ones embracing the camera as a tool for experimenting with identity as young adults. Alice Austen, who lived from 1866 to 1952, produced a large body of work, and some of her earlier photos represented experimentation with gender. Later she met Gertrude Tate, her lifelong partner, experienced disapproval from Tate family members for their "wrong devotion," and made multiple trips to Europe.[52] By the time of their first trip together in 1903, Austen had been using photography to explore place, time, and relationships for almost thirty years. Austen, the only child of a single mother from a prosperous Staten Island family, photographed her friends, her house (called "Clear Comfort"), her travels, and New York City life during the period between the time her uncle presented her with a camera in 1876 and the beginning of the Great Depression, which left her with limited means, a transition from wealth to poverty that ended with her classified as a ward of the state. Scholars have treated Austen as both an amateur and a quasi-professional photographer. In her younger years, her family's wealth allowed her to experiment with the new technology without having to make a living from it, but she did sell some photos and even had some copyrighted.

The historian Laura Wexler's perceptive reading of Austen's work highlights three important observations. First, Wexler notes that Austen's photos of "street types"—an ethnographic, photojournalistic project Austen copyrighted in 1896—treat their working-class subjects with lots of empty space around them, a distancing mechanism which demonstrates that Austen's sympathy for her subjects was far from complete. Second, she argues that the photos that play with gendered relationships "fit comfortably within ... [a] subversive tradition" identified by Jonathan Weinberg as "an entire line of American photographic reconstructions of gender from F. Holland Day to the pornographic photographic scrapbooks of Carl Van Vechten." Wexler's third observation interprets Austen's relationship to the past and the future as a striving to reconcile one with the other: "In many of her images she seems to have been trying to escape or avert a disaster she sensed was coming. Austen trusted photography as a means of stopping time. But using her camera to record and explore domestic vision did not enable her to discover what was wrong." Austen's photographic efforts, in other words, offered an illusion of control over "her world" as it changed, as Staten Island became more urban, as more immigrants and "street types" dominated the city, and as the imperialist project failed to fully ennoble the white upper-middle-class society seen as destined to take the lead in shaping a future of progress. Austen's observation about the Staten Island Cricket Club, founded in 1872, that "this is not going to be a cricket club, some day, and I'm going to have pictures of how it looks now" situates her work in the tradition of record photography, the efforts of amateur photographers to document the built landscape as it inevitably disappears behind progress.[53] Wexler's interpretation is an accurate one, and it depicts Austen as both pioneer photographer and hand-wringing late Victorian. To build upon this nuanced conception of Austen's work, we also have to consider another set of changes that Austen and her partner must have recognized: the shift in the social conception of their relationship from "close friendship" in the late nineteenth century to "abnormal" sexual identity by 1930, a shift that may have informed the production of Austen's later travel photos. While most scholars have focused on Austen's earlier glass plate era work, her film photos—and particularly those taken on multiple trips to Europe with her partner— reveal an evolving sensibility about both American modernity and individual otherness.

Alice Austen and Gertrude Tate took regular trips to Europe together between 1903 and 1912, spending time in Austria, Hungary, Italy, France, Germany, Spain, Belgium, Holland, Sweden, Denmark, Gibraltar, and the Azores. They took a short trip from Europe to Morocco in 1909. In May 1925, despite declining financial resources, the couple traveled to

Figure 8. Photo of women walking on a street, probably in Paris in 1905. Alice Austen often photographed women in motion. Photo by Alice Austen, 50.015.3596, Collection of Historic Richmond Town, Staten Island, New York.

Puerto Rico. Austen, now using film, produced a photographic record of the trips and recorded the circumstances of each photo, continuing her habit of systematic scientific note-keeping on light, distance, and conditions. The dominant themes Wexler identified in Austen's glass plate, Staten Island–focused phase hold true in her international travel photography: an interest in "street types" (with lots of space around the subjects), markets, architecture, and urban life. In the travel and film phase of Austen's work, however, one notes a growing sensibility that situated and centralized women in the activity about them. In her travels, Austen took photos of working men and women—vendors in the markets, agricultural workers, street cleaners, fishermen, and such—but her focus on women amidst motion or in motion stands out. Images of any kind of movement were not easily produced with early film cameras, so her effort to capture the motion of women in particular is noteworthy. Her preference for subjects that evoke motion reflected her own lifelong appreciation of and attraction to movement as a former athlete and the partner of a dance instructor. One photo, taken in France in September 1905, centers three women in white bonnets walking quickly, their feet far apart as a result of their long strides, with their full skirts and shawls trailing behind them from the rapidity of their movement. The city line and rows of barrels are their stationary backdrop, a contrast to their ambulation. A lone kerchief-wearing woman, stooped from age or the weight of her basket, provides another antithesis to the activity and purpose of the women in the foreground.[54]

Another photo from this same trip highlights the motion of women and provides a study in class contrast as well. The image features a woman in fashionable modern dress on the street striding toward but soon to pass the photographer on the camera's right (figure 8). Wearing white gloves and holding a book, the woman has partially obscured her face with a white scarf, but her eyes look straight ahead, purposeful, resolute, and unconcerned with the photographer. At the center of the shot, just beyond the fashionable woman, two women with fuller skirts, shawls, bonnets, and a basket stride in the other direction, away from the camera, their feet blurred slightly by the motion of walking. The class contrast is striking, as the "modern" woman and the "peasant" women (according to the logic of street types photography) inhabit the same frame but travel in opposite directions.[55] An earlier 1903 photo features a similar class contrast, showing three figures, one a fashionably dressed "modern" woman casually walking down a cobblestone street as two more traditionally dressed figures lean forward in the same direction under the weight of bags. The contrast here is not direction but speed and leisure, as the fashionable woman's stride is so small that it almost appears as if she is standing still, while the figures burdened with bags take bigger steps and lean more purposefully in the direction of their stride.[56]

Even where Austen's female subjects were not moving, the elements of the photo suggested only a slight pause in their motion and at the same time emphasized the relationship of the subject to her surroundings. One pose occurs so often that it is likely Austen coached her subjects. Figures repeatedly appear with their bodies in profile but their heads turned to glance toward the photographer, and they frequently carry some item indicating they had been engaged in labor, particularly, in the case of locals, baskets. In Innsbruck in 1905, Austen photographed a woman and a boy in this sideways pose, the woman squinting in the sun that highlights her dress, her basket, and her likeness to the boy. The road figures largely in the photo, implying the connection between the subjects and their environment.[57] She photographed two girls in a similar pose at the edge of a photo of a clock tower in Innsbruck, situating the girls in their architectural surroundings.[58] Austen captured another body-in-profile pose on a street in Capri in 1906, centralizing a woman with a basket on her head surrounded by children, other women, and buildings, one of which prominently features the word "Kodak" over a typical Kodak dealer storefront, placing the native figures in their tourist town. The contrast between the basket on the woman's head and the very modern photographic logo must have been engaging to the photographer.[59] In Tangier in 1909, Austen photographed a woman whose face is in profile while her body faces the photographer (an inversion of the scripted pose she so often used), but the key theme of the photo is the naturalness of the woman and the other figures in the city. Taken from a hilltop looking down at both the figures and the city, this image showing the expanse of Tangier and the reiteration of similar buildings emphasizes the connectedness of people and place.[60]

Austen did not reserve this association for locals, though, as she naturalized tourists as part of the landscape at the same time that she made note of their differences from locals. While her photo record of these trips included the typical tourist landscapes and ruins, she also documented tourist culture: ships, cars, tour guides, and even a postcard shop in Lourdes.[61] Most of the frame of the 1909 Lourdes photo is taken up by the street, which runs diagonally across the picture, which shows a series of tourist shops next to one another. The whole street apparently served tourists, as the photo includes five different shops featuring postcards and souvenirs. At the center right, a group of fashionably dressed women shop for souvenirs; the store to which they are headed displays a sign that declares, "English Spoken."[62]

Through Austen's lens, the tourists are depicted no more sympathetically, and no more critically, than the photos of locals in their "natural" surroundings.[63] She took a similar approach in 1903 in Holland with an architectural shot in which the street figures prominently before a row of small buildings with consistent and unique Flemish style. Instead of capturing just the street and the buildings, she included a traveling companion (probably Tate) with her back to the camera, her head lowered, and her hands hidden in front of her as if she were looking at a guidebook or even through the lens of a Kodak Brownie: a tourist

Figure 9. All motion centers on Gertrude Tate, Paris, 1905.
Alice Austen photograph, 50.015.3595, Collection of
Historic Richmond Town, Staten Island, New York.

as a natural part of a cityscape.[64] In the couple's 1909 trip to Morocco, Austen often photographed their guide, Mustapha Saidi, who operated from the Continental Hotel in Tangier and who accompanied them on June 18 when they visited Kasaba Prison, Soko Market, and a "Bedouin village," a typical schedule for English-speaking tourists. Since her trip to Morocco was quite short (June 17–20), she probably relied heavily on the guide, who appears in photos riding donkeys with Gertrude Tate, sitting on a picnic blanket with Tate, and raising a glass with a group of tourists.[65]

Two photos from Austen's 1905 trip feature her fellow tourists in their surroundings in the body-in-profile pose and are particularly unusual snaps because of their focus on a single individual. In one, Gertrude Tate and the couple's older traveling companion stand at the center on a street in France, probably in Paris (figure 9). All around the women is male motion: a bearded man enters the scene, blurry with the activity of walking. Likewise blurry, carts fly by in the background. In the far lower left, a horse hoof presages that its owner will shortly enter the scene just behind the women. The traveling companion, probably the woman identified as Mrs. Sharp in the notes accompanying the set of negatives, stands in her old-fashioned ruffled travel dress, looking skeptically at Gertrude Tate, who smiles broadly at the woman, as if enjoying a joke Mrs. Sharp did not find funny. Tate's pose is straight, relaxed, and confident (perhaps reflecting her dance training), the folds in her dress sharply focused, in contrast to the motion around her. The male activity around Tate leaves her unconcerned, as she inhabits and enjoys her own space on the street. Unlike the images of female motion—the girls in bonnets—or of an implied pause in motion suggested in Austen's photos of local women, this snapshot blurs all motion except the laughter of Austen's life partner, which is in clear focus.[66] The collection of European photos has a more narrowed sense of insiders and an expanded sense of outsiders than Austen's home photography, which featured many more photos of different subjects in her social circle.[67] Like her earlier glass plate work, Austen's film photography in Europe featured domestic or intimate scenes with friends: photos of meals, shipboard activities, even a bathroom selfie.[68] But the experience of traveling with Tate made it necessary for Austen to focus these domestic snaps more on a single person, reflecting the narrowing of their social circle but also perhaps the freedom that travel provided the couple away from family members who disapproved of their relationship. Austen could both literally and figuratively focus on her partner when away from the Tate family's surveillance. Unlike Grace Franklin, who often referred affectionately to "my hubby" without picturing him and could count on those around her to validate the relationship, Austen expressed her relationship in visual and subtle terms in her travel photography. Unlike the Franklins' "Friend Tibbal," who flirted publicly with the local girls with his safety assumed, Austen had to travel with more circumspection about the couple's "wrong devotion."

Professional and amateur photographs depicting affection between men on vacations or at leisure entered the archive at the same time as those of married heterosexual couples. Sometimes meant as private witness to relationships that had to be kept out of the public eye, the photographs attest to vacation—particularly the beach trip—as a time and place for a bit of freedom to embrace. The art historian and curator of the 2001 exhibit *Dear Friends: American Photography and Male*

Figure 10. Portrait of writer and activist Ida B. Wells-Barnett. Wells and other African American activists strategically employed their images in their work. Ida B. Wells Papers, University of Chicago Library, Special Collections Research Center.

Affection, 1840–1918, David Deitcher notes that seaside vacation settings were common in photographs depicting male affection. An 1890 tintype reproduced in the exhibit catalog shows two men in bathing suits with their arms around each other, their legs intertwined. The suit jacket of one of the men is unbuttoned at the center, showing his skin, while their beach hats lie at their feet. The image depicts affection but also excitement and the exuberance of physical recreation. The painted canvas backdrop shows a shoreline, trees, and a resort building. In another example from 1905, two men sit close together on a bench, one with his arm around the other. The painted canvas backdrop shows ocean waves and a sign reading "Sea Breeze."[69] Such seaside portraits were common at late nineteenth- and early twentieth-century beach resorts, but for men creating queer identities in this period, the portrait studio may have been a safer place to take candid photos, even in resort areas that would be identified with gay clientele. Tourist photography in this case could subject its sitters to severe penalties, social, economic, and legal, which led to circumspection in public places. Such unequal access to public space limited not only the freedom of gay tourists but also the creation of archives, which constrained gay men's and lesbians' access to the national historical narrative that such archives enabled.

Around the same time that Alice Austen and others were beginning the photographic archive of queer life in the United States, African American photographers were building on a long history of using the camera in creating a social memory that focused on the art, work, and cultural ties of African American individuals and communities. As the groundbreaking photographic historian Deborah Willis has demonstrated, African American professional photographers ran successful businesses from the beginnings of commercial and artistic photography in the United States in the 1840s, and went on to shape every major movement in both.[70] In the period before the First World War, photographers like J. P. Ball, the Goodridge brothers Glenalvin, William, and Wallace, George O. Brown, and Daniel Freeman documented the people and events of African American communities across the nation, providing a counter to the racist stereotypes dominant in white visual culture and modeling photographic behaviors for an emerging generation of Black hobby photographers.[71] J. P. Ball is especially notable as an early model of a photographic professional, for not only did a diversity of clientele seek his work, but also he facilitated a public exhibition, *Ball's Splendid Mammoth Pictorial Tour of the United States, Comprising Views of the African Slave Trade; of Northern and Southern Cities; of Cotton and Sugar Plantations; of the Mississippi, Ohio and Susquehanna Rivers &C*, a panorama shown in his Cincinnati studio in 1855.[72] Black activists and intellectuals like Frederick Douglass, Paul Laurence Dunbar, W. E. B. Du Bois, and Ida B. Wells (figure 10) provided additional models, as they embraced the potential of photography to offer evidence that African American people were not what they were purported to be by white stereotypes.[73]

As consumers, African Americans drew on photography to reflect nuanced and diverse identities, but Kodak rarely marketed specifically to Black consumers.[74] Of the 549 ads promoting Kodak products in the Hartman Center for Sales, Advertising, and Marketing History digital collections, none pictured African Americans as camera users.[75] Black newspapers regularly carried stories about and advertisements for different types of cameras. In 1886 the *Cleveland Gazette* ran a story about film photography, explaining that "an apparatus is now produced which enables a tourist to make hundreds of photographs without even the trouble of putting in and taking out a glass plate."[76] Multiple issues of *The Freeman* in the 1890s carried an advertisement for the handheld "Comet" camera which pointed out the connection between photography and tourism, noting that "travelers and tourists use it to obtain a picturesque diary of their travels" while "ocean travelers use it to photograph fellow passengers on steamships."[77] The Black press covered cameras and picture taking regularly, with stories of trick cameras, the camera habits of tourists, and technological innovations appearing throughout the late nineteenth and early twentieth centuries, often addressing the close relationship between travel and photography.[78] This public dialogue, by referring to the photographic activities of Black activists who were controlling their images and engaging in travel, encouraged others who could afford these leisure pursuits to take them up.

As scholars of Black photography have shown, for the period before World War I, the bulk of the photographic record of African American life comes from studios and communities: family portraits, individual portraits, and images of religious activities, school activities, and public celebrations like Emancipation Day.[79] The photography represented the general trend of post-emancipation efforts in building institutions and stabilizing place-based communities. Travel did appear as a theme in this period, but it looked very different from the leisure travel of wealthy whites. African Americans traveled to visit family, for military service, and for work, and the photographic record reflects these themes. Black soldiers posed for studio portraits in military uniforms, probably before leaving for duty or to communicate with family members at home.[80] The writer Edward P. Jones, in a poignant essay about a photograph taken in a Washington, DC, studio of his mother as a young woman, notes that the Great Migration increased the importance of family photos and allowed family members to maintain ties with loved ones. In his account of the role of photos in family history, he observes that those who migrated

> did not find in the North as much as God had promised them in their dreams. But what they did find, they wanted to document, since it was so often so much more than what they had had "back home" in the South. And one way of documenting it was in photos. Black men and women, workers in the Detroit car plants, in the Chicago stockyards, in the mansions of Washington politicians, had pictures taken of themselves sitting on the hoods or in the driver's seats of cars they were still paying for, dressed in exquisite clothes they would not have minded being buried in. Some had their own cameras, but others, like my mother, visited photography shops. They all sent pictures "back home," back to relatives who stuck

them in the frames of cracked mirrors or put them away in dresser drawers lest the strong light of the South fade the pictures and take away their magic; back to relatives who marveled over the changes in sons and daughters and cousins.[81]

Jones had come into possession of the photo of his mother when a relative from North Carolina gave it to him after his mother's death, attesting to the geographic dynamics of studio portraits. Even before the Great Migration, travel as a theme sometimes appeared in studio photographs of African Americans. The photographer recorded only as "Photographed by Black" captured a studio image of an African American teenager sitting on a suitcase. This image, which predated the Kodak by perhaps twenty years, shapes the subject as a person on the move. The youth wears a coat buttoned to the top and a cap and is seated on the case with his left leg on his right knee. The painted backdrop shows a lake or river scene. The young man's expression is plaintive, as if he is exercising patience in sitting for the photo. The collector categorized the photo under "servants," but the exact circumstances of this photographic moment can only be conjectured.[82]

African Americans exercised mobility despite Jim Crow and the white violence that enforced it. From 1865 to 1890, Americans quadrupled the length of railroad track available to travelers, and as the leisure historian Cindy Aron has shown, this increase played a significant role in the "democratization of travel" in the late nineteenth century.[83] Paired with the expansion of white-collar employment—which was increasingly adopting the regular vacation as a way to heighten productivity—railroads promoted the growth of resorts by allowing working people an easier way to get from the city to various spas, lakes, and ocean locations. A few railroads even created resorts to ensure consistent ticket purchases along the routes.[84] African Americans participated actively in the burgeoning new leisure practices, and whites responded by imposing social and legal limits. The historian Mark Foster notes that when African American vacationers organized large group outings to the Gulf of Mexico in the late nineteenth century, "the presence of significant numbers of well-dressed Blacks enjoying themselves offended some whites, who pressured the railroads to enforce state segregation laws."[85] As the historian Blair L. M. Kelley demonstrated in her study of African American community organization against streetcar segregation, Black riders consistently pushed back against unequal access to transportation, leading to the suit brought by Homer Plessy against railcar segregation, an action that ended with the Supreme Court decision in *Plessy v. Ferguson,* which upheld the "separate but equal" doctrine and solidified Jim Crow in the United States.[86] Not only did law and custom force African Americans to sit in separate cars (the central issue in *Plessy*), but also they were required to use separate waiting rooms, bathrooms, and ticket counters at rail depots. Rail travel became a highly visible tool for and symbol of enacting white privilege. As Jim Crow strengthened in the late nineteenth and early twentieth centuries, its restrictions focused on enforcing inequity in four main areas of American life: voting, work, education, and leisure. African Americans fought against discrimination in public spaces of leisure, from restaurants and hotels to swimming pools, beaches, midways, and roller rinks. Whites responded violently, making leisure practice a battleground for white supremacy and freedom in tourist snapshotting a risky endeavor for African Americans.[87]

Steamship travel, which involved months of transit and long stays in foreign countries, remained inaccessible for most African Americans in the late nineteenth and early twentieth centuries, but many who did travel accessed it in a professional capacity or for activism. African Americans who found steamship travel economically feasible also discovered foreign travel could be a mixed bag, with travelers not knowing if they would be met with fair and courteous treatment or humiliation. Mark Foster, in studying the published travel narratives of prominent African Americans going abroad, learned that a number experienced a sense of freedom, for even if Europeans often considered them "exotic," they sometimes found relief from the overt markers of Jim Crow shaping American travel infrastructure. At other times, workers and guests at hotels would treat Black travelers with disdain, and Black tourists would discover that their reserved rooms or tables were suddenly unavailable when they showed up.[88] William Pickens, an educator traveling with his wife in Europe in 1913, nevertheless found that encountering racist white Americans abroad could be part of the entertainment, because these white tourists traveled with their racism but were not supported abroad by the infrastructure of Jim Crow. Pickens wrote:

> Not all American white people are alike, but it is noteworthy that on all this journey during all these months the only snobs we met, were some of our fellow-Americans. . . . Being far from Mississippi

and Texas, they could not work their will, but they often showed their manners anyhow, just from sheer force of habit. . . . Whenever any one glared as we entered a dining-room, or tried to spread himself out over three or four seats when we entered a vehicle, we knew where he was from. And those who made the biggest scenes, proved, on investigation, to be from the section of the United States where they are *most used to colored folk,* where from infancy they sit in the laps and eat out of the hands of black people. If a fellow was from Mississippi, where he had slept in the bed and suckled at the breast of a black nurse, he made the biggest fuss of anybody. Some of it was ludicrous. We had great fun.[89]

Even if the experience of European leisure was economically not within the reach of a vast majority of African Americans, the travel narratives produced by Pickens and other notable Black intellectuals like W. E. B. Du Bois, Mary Church Terrell, Booker T. Washington, and Langston Hughes made travel a key feature of African American public discourse and often included discussions of the ways in which travel gave new insight on (and some relief from) racism and American race relations. Such a dialogue laid the groundwork for increasing use of portable amateur photography among African Americans by the 1920s.

Between the release of the Kodak in 1888 and the beginning of the First World War, Americans embraced cameras en masse, but individual users' choices within the visual-spatial complex of travel photography were diverse and heavily informed by systems of privilege and oppression that structured the public spaces designated as tourist sites. Guided by their experiences with professional photographers in portrait studios, a tradition of public dialogue about travel, and the instructions of the Kodak Company, camera users embraced the personal visual legacy machine as an opportunity to question or support those systems (or both) from their own perspectives. Their association of cameras with mobility informed their attempts to make meaning of their participation as the country took its first steps toward full engagement in the First World War.

Chapter Four

"WHEN I SEND YOU A PICTURE OF BERLIN"

The Memory Emergency of the First World War

By the time the United States entered the First World War in 1917, the country had experienced thirty years of associating the portable camera with travel and personal archiving. Americans as a whole had little direct experience of the horrors of the war, and they drew on familiar themes—like tourism and travel—to help explain or assuage the disruption. Kodak, never one to miss a cultural beat, applied its touristic themes explicitly to military travel. A 1917 *Saturday Evening Post* ad used the "Take a Kodak with you" tagline, but instead of picturing cars, trains, or tourist scenes as in the company's earlier marketing, it featured a group of uniformed soldiers developing film at a military camp. The perspective is from inside a tent, looking out at the men, whose focus is on the developed film. A man with a cigar in his mouth is holding the film as the other, younger men smile. The scene is congenial and pleasant, more like a camping trip than an experience of war.[1] Another 1917 ad drew even closer connections between war and tourism. Captioned "The Kodak Story of the War," it includes an illustration of a sailor posing on a ship while a friend records his image (figure 11). The text asserts: "War isn't all fighting—but to thousands of young Americans on shipboard and in camp it will be a new world, will open up a new life. . . . The daily routine on shipboard and in camp, the shore leave in strange cities, the pictures of comrades—all these things will make a heart-gripping Kodak story."[2]

Kodak was certainly not alone in framing the war as an opportunity for adventure and travel. In 1918, the songwriters Frank Fay, Ben Ryan, and Dave Dreyer issued sheet music for the exceptionally catchy "When I Send You a Picture of Berlin (You Know It's Over 'Over There,' I'm Coming Home)," which told the story of Johnny Johnson, a "cam'ra fiend," who, because he was leaving as a soldier, was finally getting to fulfill his dream of photographing the great cities of Europe:

> Johnny Johnson feeling fit, uniform and army kit
> Johnny was a cam'ra fiend, of that trip he'd often dreamed
> Sweetheart crying at the pier, said "I'm proud of you my dear
> Now you'll realize your dreams, taking pictures of those scenes."
> Said John that's what I'll do, and I'll send them home to you.
> [Chorus]
> When I send you a picture of London, then you'll know I've landed
>   safely "Over There"
> When I send you a snapshot of Paris, you'll know I'm ready to do and
>   dare (I'll do my share)
> You'll know I'm thinking about you, when I send you my photo all
>   alone
> But when I send you a picture of Berlin, you'll know it's over "Over
>   There" I'm coming home

Johnny's photographic romp through the great cities of Europe sounded like great fun in the first chorus of "When I Send You a Picture of Berlin," and the second chorus assured listeners that all soldiers were like him and that those at home just had to wait a bit until the inevitable victory:

> Sweetheart waving at the pier, saw the transport disappear
> Dried her tears and heaved a sigh, said he'll come back "bye and bye"
> There are millions more like him, full of vim and fighting trim

The Kodak Story of the War.

War isn't all fighting—but to thousands of young Americans on shipboard and in camp it will be a new world, will open up a new life. New ties will be formed, new friendships cemented. The daily routine on shipboard and in camp, the shore leave in strange cities, the pictures of comrades—all these things will make a heart gripping Kodak story for the folks at home.

It's a genuine part of the Nation's present job to keep tight the bonds between its fighters and those at home who can follow only with their hearts. Pictures from home and to the home can do their part.

There's room for a little Vest Pocket KODAK in every sailor's and soldier's kit. The expense is small, six dollars. The cheerfulness it may bring is great. They are on sale by Kodak dealers, everywhere.

EASTMAN KODAK COMPANY, ROCHESTER, N. Y.

Figure 11. "The Kodak Story of the War," Kodak advertisement, 1917, Emergence of Advertising in America Collection, John W. Hartman Center for Sales, Advertising, and Marketing History, Rubenstein Library, Duke University.

Smiling when they sail away, our debt to France they're glad to pay
We'll miss them all at home, but there's truth in Johnny's poem
[Chorus]

The cover art, trimmed in red, white, and blue, shows Johnny in his uniform with an extremely large and hardly portable-looking telescoping camera, gazing intently at his subject (figure 12). He stands in the rounded inset within a battle scene featuring soldiers on horses carrying an inordinate number of American flags as they charge through the Brandenburg Gate.[3] In May 1918, Arthur Fields and the Peerless Quartet recorded the snappy tune, issuing it through Victor.[4]

The insistence of fictional Johnny and his family on framing his experience as a tourist trip through Europe seems exceptionally naïve, given the trauma, dislocation, and horror brought on by the war, but because of their geographic isolation, Americans had not fully comprehended the brutality of the war in Europe. From a visual perspective, much of what soldiers' families saw of their departures looked like a mobility similar to that of tourism and vacation, as they packed their bags, their documents, and their cameras and boarded trains to leave for mobilization centers. Even as Arthur Fields and the Peerless Quartet sang happily of Johnny's picture-taking opportunities, soldiers and their families used cameras to ease the pain of separation and worry, to commemorate historic events, and, sometimes, to remember the dead. A photo, they realized, might be family members' last sight of their fighting young. In this way, the First World War strengthened the archival imperative started by tourism to document experiences and arrange the visual evidence in albums, scrapbooks, and frames. War-related deaths, as well as the demographic disaster of the flu epidemic in 1918–19, made the documentation and memorialization of life an even stronger impulse. Like the Civil War generation's taking up scrapbooking to work through ideas about life, death, and nationalism, participation in such an important global event inspired camera marketers and advertisers to explicitly connect individual experience to national and international history.[5] The First World War had created a memory emergency that amplified the imperatives of the mass production of memory.

At the end of the first volume of the *Cambridge History of World War I*, the historian Jay Winter offers an engaging essay titled "Picturing War." The piece leads the reader through a diverse collection of photographs taken during World War I, primarily by professional photographer-

Figure 12. "When I Send You a Picture of Berlin," sheet music cover, Library of Congress, Music Division.

correspondents. The photos, Winter notes, represent the transnational, the strange, the unexpected, and the horrific. The collection includes images of prisoners of war from African and Asian countries of the French Empire, a Serbian soldier lying on the ground in the transition to death, soldiers scaling mountains and sailors floating in the sea, and even a grisly photo of a partial horse carcass rotting in a treetop. Winter writes that photos provide a kind of understanding not possible through other sources: "Photography is part of the essential documentation of war. Its strength is to have captured moments—moments of horror or wonder, or just a sense of the uncanny mix of the familiar and the bizarre. The portability of the camera created vast public archives, enabling us to escape from official photography, and to have a glimpse of the enormous character of war from the standpoint of the observer, the person captivated by . . . the shock of recognition at seeing not clichés and stereotypes, but traces of the strange face of war itself."[6] The power of the image to disrupt the banal and the familiar is well known, but scholars also have much to gain in the study of "clichés and stereotypes." Citizens of the United States often evoked formulaic images in their photographs of and public dialogue about the First World War. The Eastman Kodak Company's advertising played a major role in managing the meanings of mass photography in both peace and war, and its aggressive advertising of the Kodak's role in the war not only brought on a period of increased sales of cameras, film, and albums but also provided a model for making meaning from war experiences. Pervasive Kodak marketing, military efforts to control camera use by soldiers, and the stresses of war on families all led to the proliferation of war photos that looked a great deal like tourist photos. Such selective memory making in the context of familial disruption, psychological distancing from violence, and the advertising industry's cultural influence reveals that the ability of mass photography to order and arrange is indeed as powerful as its ability to disrupt.

Soldiers and sailors used photos to communicate with their families during long absences from home and also to document service to the war effort. As Inge Hennemen notes in the exhibition catalog for *Shooting Range*, an exhibition of First World War photographs at the FotoMuseum of Antwerp, "Between front and homefront, photographic portraits and snapshots from the brusquely divided worlds emigrated in great numbers."[7] As in other countries on either side of the war, the most common amateur photo related to US military service was the uniform photo, an image of the serviceman standing in uniform, either on leave at home or taking a break elsewhere. While some soldiers and sailors posed for formal studio portraits, most just posed for cameras held by family members and friends. Sailor Dean T. Tarvin of Illinois was photographed in his uniform in front of the Illinois Café, while airman Carl R. Smith is seen casting a shadow late in the day in front of a large brick house with white columns.[8] Charles Gibson stands casually in his army uniform, leaning on a portable camp building.[9] Ernest B. Ricks posed in camp looking ready to march with his rifle, ammunition, and canteen, which produced a photo that was later trimmed into an oval and pasted into an album.[10] Clarence H. Dickey, a twenty-eight-year-old auto mechanic from Clinton, Illinois, joined the army in 1918 and fought in the battles at Saint-Mihiel and the Argonne. It was probably during downtime in France when he posed in his uniform, wearing his wedding ring, and holding his rifle in front of a building.[11] The ubiquity of person-in-place poses and distance shots of damage to the built environment can partially be explained by the cultural association of the camera with tourism but should also be understood in terms of feasibility. For security reasons, the military discouraged individual soldiers' camera use and provided official photos from the Signal Corps to media and other outlets. Just as the military screened letters to eliminate exposure of sensitive information, it also monitored photos sent home, resulting in a limited archive of personal photographs. A desire among soldiers to spare their loved ones worry also determined the types of photos taken during the war. Finally, leave time provided more opportunity for taking pictures, contributing to an archive of photos that look like tourist shots. The Young Men's Christian Association played a significant role in managing leave time, an effort supported by military leaders looking to keep soldiers out of trouble. It functioned like an excursion company, booking whole hotels and arranging sightseeing tours.[12] The photos from these excursions fed the association of war with tourism.

Veterans' memory practices included not just photos and albums but also eventually local histories. Arthur Lloyd Fletcher, as part of the History Committee of the 113th Field Artillery, Thirtieth Division, wrote a 262-page history of the 113th published in 1920. He included a hefty dose of statistics, timelines, and maps, but central to the history was a narrative that drew heavily on the conventions of the upper-middle-class turn-of-the-century travel narrative as well as the travel photo album. Like a travel narrative, the history included amusing anecdotes about linguistic and cultural differences as well as descriptions of preparations, the ocean crossing, foreign food, places, activities, and the return voyage. Like the travel photo album, it contained snapshots taken by the participants, each with its own caption. Fletcher included a photo collage to explain the division's training at Camp Sevier in South Carolina, which showed group shots and individual shots of soldiers taking breaks in their training, their tents in snow and sun, and even a snapshot of Danger the pit bull mascot standing at attention.[13]

Photos of ruined infrastructure look quite similar in composition to engravings of ruins in nineteenth-century travel narratives.[14] In her essay for the exhibit catalog *The Great War: The Persuasive Power of Photography*, Ann Thomas notes that during the First World War, professional photographers also used the pictorial and the picturesque approaches traditionally employed in photographing ruins.[15] Such approaches provided the visual accompaniment to travel narratives, a tradition continued in some of the amateur histories of the war. In Fletcher's *History of the 113th Field Artillery, 30th Division*, one caption of a hilltop view of Verdun explicitly connects to tourism: "Many officers and men of the regiment visited this famous town after the Armistice." The caption under a photo of a house with men posing in front evokes the rarified language of architectural tourism by describing the subject as the "beautiful log bungalow used as regimental headquarters." Only of a few of the photos included in Fletcher's history reveal the visual evidence of battle, the kinds of photos Jay Winter would consider as going beyond the "clichés and stereotypes" of the memory of the First World War: one of a funeral, one of a cemetery, and two of explosions. In her study of photo albums made by First World War veterans, Janina Struk found that while soldiers did take snapshots of disturbing scenes—even when expressly forbidden to do so by the armed forces—veterans kept them more private, which in part explains why quasi-public histories like the *History of the 113th* included so few images of disturbing scenes. Another explanation, at least in the context of the United States, is that camera advertising emphasized that photography was meant for recording the happiness of life, not its horrors.[16]

Eastman Kodak urged loved ones to use the camera to maintain communication between home and the front: "Keep your Kodak busy for the sake of the lads in the trenches," advises a 1918 ad featuring a group of clean, healthy young men in uniform sharing pictures enclosed in letters from home, reinforcing the centrality of the camera in boosting morale.[17] A version of this ad for Christmas 1917 highlights a group of soldiers looking at a photo; the gift of a Kodak at Christmas would allow the user to "make light hearts and happy faces by sending a continued Kodak story . . . to the brave lads, somewhere in France."[18] Kodak's claim that the camera was crucial to morale had official backing. In 1918, W. Frank Persons, director of civilian relief for the American Red Cross, told the *New York Times* that photos from home would fortify soldiers against shell shock and urged those on the home front to document life fully and share it with soldiers: "Our soldiers cannot come home for visits . . . therefore . . . we must take the American home to them—must keep them constantly in touch with American life as we are living it from day to day in city, town, or rural district."[19] Kodak emphasized the return of the soldiers and only obliquely referenced the possibility that some might not come back. The text of the 1917 "Before He Goes" ad emphasized the eventual triumphant return of the soldiers and the duty of those at home to use photos to lift the spirits of the troops. The image is of a couple: he in uniform holding a small child, while she takes their portrait. The meaning of this image paired with the tagline "Before He Goes" could not have been lost on families facing separation and the possible loss of a young father.[20]

A less emotional marketing approach drew directly on the idea of photography as an instrument of historical science. "Jerusalem Regained," an ad appearing in *Country Gentleman* in 1918, emphasized what it presented as the continuity of Anglo-Western power in the arc of history. Next to a drawing of returned English Crusaders showing off treasures of the Holy Land appears a photographic reproduction of British soldiers in the First World War marching into Jerusalem. While the continuity of empire comes through visually, the text makes an important distinction between the two situations: the method through which the events were recorded and whereby they will be assessed as history by future generations. While the Crusaders' exploits are remembered in "fragments of song and legend that we must [use to] piece together our picture of that crowning triumph of medieval chivalry," the modern soldiers' efforts will be documented more scientifically and more accurately because of photography: "Yesterday a soldier of Britain set the flag of Empire over the Holy City's temples, mosques, and battlements. And close on the heels of the news came photographic confirmation as precise as Allenby's own uncolored reports to the War Office. Thus today does history record itself while in the making, almost automatically. Largely because of photography, today's hero tales can never recede into the mists of folklore; the story told by photographs remains authentic, even through another thousand years."[21] The ad is remarkable in its claims that technology objectively records, seemingly without the bias of a human being. It goes on to assert additional scientific objectivity by claiming that "the Eastman Kodak Company, like a great university . . . constantly renders the world a real institutional service."[22] A similar ad in the *Saturday Evening Post* in 1918 compared Kodak's contributions to war photography to those of Matthew Brady in the US Civil War, though unlike Brady, "trundling his horse-drawn darkroom from battlefield to battlefield," modern Kodak users can "make scores of snap-shots in the time Brady needed to obtain a single 'view.'" The corporation, according to this ad, held a great deal of responsibility in compiling history: "Thus do current war pictures form a chapter of history as yet in the writing. Long after we have won the war, other generations may still see today's battles refought across the screen; and in the march of science which makes such wonders possible, we trust it will be vouchsafed the Eastman Kodak Company to maintain, as in the past, its high traditions of service and leadership."[23] The recording imperative extended from the corporation to the individual in a time of war. A 1917 ad showing an illustration of a woman giving a Vest Pocket Kodak to a parting soldier emphasizes the soldier's role in recording history. First the ad points out that times of "forced inaction" in soldiers' lives—"It is monotony, not bullets that our soldier boys dread"—could be filled with picture taking, an activity that would allow doughboys to record "a story that will always be intense to them because it is *history* from their view-point. And when peace comes it will make more vivid, more real *their story of the war* as they tell it again and again to mother and sister and wife and little ones."[24]

Such recording had its limits, however. A *Kodak Trade Circular* article titled "Cameras for Soldiers" told dealers that George Creel, chair of the federal government's Committee on Public Information, had informed the Kodak Company that cameras would not be allowed in the trenches, a detail not revealed in advertising.[25] Even professional photographers faced difficulties in documenting the war, for, as Jane Carmichael found in her study of professional photographers during the First World War, the "camera was a not uncommon part of the personal 'kit' taken to war but attitudes toward its use varied. Private cameras were equated with the keeping of diaries as being a possible security risk on active service and were therefore officially frowned on. Several attempts were made to ban them altogether," but none were fully successful in keeping the portable camera out of the line of fire.[26]

The ubiquity of the camera can be partly explained by its popularity in domestic life, and the First World War presented a unique moment in which to sell cameras by associating travel, memory, and history. Kodak instructed its dealers to take advantage of the significant business opportunity. A *Kodak Trade Circular* article in the June 1914 edition, titled "If War Comes," noted that in the event of war, "an immense body of men should at once be moved to strategic points. . . . Practically all these men are young men, eager to do and to see the wonders of a strange country." Dealers should advise these men, "'Take a Kodak with you.' Secure a list of the names and addresses of every member of every military organization within your trade limits, and have prepared, ready to send out on short notice, a letter embodying the above suggestion." To help the dealers, the circular provided a sample letter alerting future doughboys about their impending photographic needs: "You will witness many strange and interesting sights, and take part in events that will become history. You will surely want more than a mental impression and we know you will welcome our suggestion that you 'take a Kodak with you.'"[27] By January 1915, Kodak recognized that "European travel is out of the question" but noted that tourists would be spending their travel dollars at home, and optimism ran high: "1915 is going to be a big Kodak year—the biggest ever."[28] The company invested heavily in marketing its new autographic Kodak (which let users record written information right on the film), employing war themes in its advertising, and in September 1917 the *Kodak Trade Circular* was flush with the company's wartime success: "Business has already felt the war time demand for photographs. Stimulated by our advertising, it is breaking all records."[29] By the end of 1917, the company was holding fast to the hard sell during wartime, instructing dealers to "drive it home at every opportunity that Kodak pictures with their sentiment and heart tingles are the greatest gifts the soldiers and sailor boys can receive."[30]

Kodak appealed to women's domestic obligations as family historians in a 1919 ad, "The Day That Will Never Come Again," which appeared in *Leslie's Weekly*, picturing an elderly man talking to a woman recording on an autographic Kodak as the returning troops—"Eyes front and chins up, crusaders all, hardened veterans in a glorious cause"—march by their window in the background. The text instructs the presumably female reader on the importance of the day beyond her own feelings:

You thrill with great love, a love of country and a love for the men who have saved the world. This day marks an epoch whose events you are privileged to witness; it a day that will never come again.... Pictures from your point of vantage—just as you saw it—that recall the glory and greatness of it all—these will keep it fresh and vivid, will bring back the thrill and breathless glow.... And on each negative you may have, not merely the picture story, but the date and title, the full authentic history—with an Autographic Kodak.

While the ad depended on the female reader's sense of her obligation to record family history, hence a domestic duty, it connected those recording duties to the scientific, "masculine" history of the nation and the changes over time in nation-states. The autographic Kodak made the supposed scientific accuracy of the photograph even more compelling by offering the consumer the opportunity to inscribe it with text, a label to help convey meaning "when memory alone can scarce recall the scene."[31]

Although soldiers may have been limited in their ability to record their activities and relay their experiences to others via the photograph, other participants in the war effort had a bit more freedom. Emma Y. Dickson, a YMCA canteen worker from a wealthy Montclair, New Jersey, family, arrived in France in April 1918 and returned to New Jersey from her final post in Germany in February 1919. In almost a year of relief work at or near the front, she kept a diary, saved news clippings, collected programs, and gathered drawings and letters from soldiers. In addition, she took photos. On her return, she combined them into a scrapbook containing a typescript diary, photos, picture postcards, letters, programs, and news clippings that combined touristic perceptions of the visual with an archiving imperative that connected individual experience to national narrative. While Dickson rarely mentioned her camera explicitly, she documented her experiences of the war in the precise ways urged by Kodak advertising.

Emma Dickson was born in Pennsylvania in 1891 into a family headed by the businessman and progressive reformer William B. Dickson, a child of immigrants and a former laborer who had risen through the ranks of United States Steel until 1914, when he left to form the Midvale Steel and Ordnance Company of New York. The Dicksons—Emma, her father, her mother, Mary, and five other siblings—lived in Montclair with at least four household servants. Educated at a private school, the recipient of tutoring in language and music, the owner of a 1916 Stutz Roadster, and an active socialite, Emma Dickson seems an unlikely candidate to sign up for a tour of serving hot chocolate to and writing letters for soldiers in World War I. Nevertheless, at age twenty-eight, inspired by her father's efforts on behalf of laborers, she applied to the YMCA to go abroad to be a canteen worker. According to accounts of family and friends, William Dickson initially opposed the idea but relented after Emma's second application was accepted. On February 26, 1918, he penned a letter on Midvale Steel and Ordnance Company letterhead stating:

> This letter is given to my daughter, Emma Y. Dickson, who is about to sail for France to engage in Relief Work. Its purpose is to serve as an additional means of identification; her photograph being attached hereto and sealed with the seal of this Company, and her signature being appended hereto. It will only be used by her in case of some unforeseen emergency arising, and any person to who [sic] she may present it with an appeal for assistance, is hereby assured that the undersigned will be responsible for any reasonable charges which may be incurred in rendering such assistance.

The head-and-shoulders identification shot shows a young woman looking not exactly pleased with the process. The Dickson patriarch's support secured, Emma Dickson left for France on the *Espagne* on April 3, 1918, for what would turn out to be almost a year of YMCA relief work at the front. While others noted that she brought both her privilege and her violin with her, less noticed were her meticulous recordkeeping skills, her typewriter—to which she referred by its brand name as "the Corona"—and her portable camera.[32]

She told of her first experiences on board the *Espagne* through tourist tropes, documenting the weather and activities aboard the ship, meeting (and photographing) the famous operatic diva Mary Garden and her large white poodle, and attending French classes. A few days out of port, she was thrilled to learn that the *Espagne* carried troops who had been staying out of sight for security reasons until the ship was well onto the open seas. After this discovery, her photos included shots of servicemen posing or engaged in games as well as group shots of Red Cross workers. The photos and captions reveal she was getting to know some details of the servicemen's lives, such as in one caption of a photo of three men that reads, "French soldier, champion wrestler and boy from Wisconsin." After arriving in France, she spent a couple of weeks exploring Paris, taking photos of Madeleine Church and the Place de la Concorde, and even attending the opera and getting her hair done. As her YMCA training continued, she wrote to her mother: "This is wonderful work they're doing over here. I have a different point of view already, and I'm sure I'll come back a much better person—and I'm gladder every day that I've had this opportunity."[33]

Leaving Paris at the end of April, she reported to William Danforth, secretary of YMCA operations in the area of Châteauvillain, continuing to display touristic sensibilities in recording her experiences: taking photos of herself in a new place, buying picture postcards, and sharing descriptions and historical facts through letters. The scrapbook related individual experiences through the lens of the tourist on a "jaunt . . . agreeable and instructive," in the words of a tourist during the first wave of mass tourism in the United States in the mid-nineteenth century. In studying this earlier generation of travelers, the historian Cindy Aron found that they framed their leisure activities as socially beneficial, as trips that could invigorate one's physical or mental health through a change of scenery, a chance to learn about institutions, history, and people.[34] In the early pages of her scrapbook, Emma Dickson used such ideas as framing devices for her experiences, even posing in Valdelancourt in the Ardennes in her clean, crisp apron with her fellow canteen workers in front of her first "Y" café. Her diary, and excerpts included in it from the diaries of her co-workers William Danforth and Helen Bagoe, reveal the thrill of serving hot chocolate at the front, sleeping outdoors, and enjoying one another's company. Even gas mask training looks like fun in the photos, and according to Bagoe, the first gas alarms were exciting: "Gas mask alarms sounded—signals flashed, and Col. Dore took us up to front line and over 'no man's land.' Wonderful experiences." They visited ruined castles, bought picture postcards, exchanged English lessons for French lessons with locals, and even collected souvenirs, like the button taken from the coat of one of the first German soldiers Dickson encountered. In a letter to her brother, she recounted the scene: "I was just coming out when the ambulance brought in a German boy. He was only 19 and had been shot in about 20 places, but he made me shiver just to look at him because he was a Boche. One of the doctors gave me a button off his coat, and I'll bring it home for you as a souvenir."[35] Dickson's switch from the formal national designation to the slur in a single sentence, and the casualness with which she speaks of collecting souvenirs from the enemy's body, indicate a continued use of tourist tropes to explain her experiences in France in her scrapbook covering the summer of 1918. Such tropes would soon become strained.

On June 29, 1918, Emma Dickson wrote a letter to her father that must have been alarming. She started by saying she could not tell him the whole story yet because "our chief, Mr. Danforth has requested us not to write home of certain incidents, as he thinks you might worry, and things always sound much worse on paper than when they are told, so many of the most interesting experiences will have to wait." She went on to include details that were acceptable under Mr. Danforth's rubric of worry assessment yet still harrowing:

> One night, we got within 4 kilometers of the Germans, and we were between the French heavy artillery and the light field artillery, which is pretty close. Everyone had to wear their gas-mask over their shoulder, to put on at a moment's notice. . . . Well, I must stop now and go over to the Hospital—about 200 gassed men have just been brought in. This is the most horrible part—they suffer so terribly, and there is so little that can be done to help. This mustard gas just burns the skin so that it comes off with their clothes.[36]

Photos of Emma Dickson and her friend Helen Bagoe amidst ruined buildings and shell holes as well as photos of wounded men toward the end of June and July's entries document the pair's experience caring for the injured at Field Hospital 26. Dickson took about eight photos of wounded soldiers being loaded into ambulances—one captioned "Ambulances pouring in to the Field Hospital 26 with their suffering burden of human wrecks"—or lying on stretchers outside, and related the nonstop work of assisting doctors, identifying the wounded, writing letters for the dying, and feeling helpless, hungry, and exhausted yet at the same time unable to eat or sleep. On July 16 she wrote, "We helped at F.H. 26, carrying coffee to the men in the ward tents and I fed one poor soul who has shell shock so terribly that his muscles contracted and I could hardly get the spoon in his mouth."[37] She included more photos of air raid destruction and one graphic photo of a "Dead German." In the July 23 diary entry that accompanied this photo, she wrote: "We got some oranges to give away which are most appreciated. The effect of the mustard gas is dreadful. How they do suffer! I feel as though my feelings were numb and that I am walking through a horrible nightmare. Helen and I wrote some letters for the men. It's hard to tell their sweethearts that they are coming back when we know they have only a few more hours to live."[38] In a July 22 letter to her sister she demonstrated her own awareness that the experiences of war had changed her: "This last week we have been working night and day at the hospital. Helen Bagoe and I have been here together, and we've seen so strenuous times. You wouldn't believe how brave I've gotten to be. I can look at these poor men all gory and torn, without turning a hair, and some of them are frightfully burned by this mustard gas, so that wherever you touch them the skin falls off." Despite such details in the written elements of her scrapbook, her photos of Field Hospital 26 are taken from a distance and do not reflect the level of intimacy Emma Dickson felt with the suffering. One was even shot from a faraway upper-story window or balcony, further distancing the suffering from the camera's lens.[39] Unlike in the earlier, more touristic photos that show people up close, the photos documenting trauma opted for space between the lens and its subject.

In the summer of 1918, in the immediate aftermath of Emma Dickson's experience of treating wounded and dying men at the Second Battle of the Marne, she took a vacation with her friend Helen Bagoe. Having received praise from their superiors and from the officers of the Third Division and the commanding officer of the field hospital, the women were given orders for two weeks' leave and promptly left for Chamonix. The scrapbook abruptly shifts to postcards, snapshots of hiking on the Mer de Glace glacier, and diary entries about taking hot baths, eating melon, and returning to "Paris again after that wonderful vacation."[40] While her scrapbook returns to documenting the day-to-day activities of a canteen worker, it also addressed mourning, including snapshots of men who died in battle, poems about loss, clippings about the deceased and the wounded, a letter from the Red Cross responding to an inquiry about a missing friend, and news items documenting the significance of the battle. In August and September she twice mentioned to her mother that she was considering coming home, but she continued working with the Third Division throughout the summer and fall, complaining of rats, interacting with German prisoners, staying with French families, and serving thousands of cups of hot chocolate.[41] In November 1918 she wrote to her mother about her impending movement with the Third Division to Germany, saying: "I've never been so well in my life as I am now, so I guess roughing it agrees with me. . . . Most of my best friends were either killed or hurt, but gradually they are drifting back from the hospitals and it keeps me busy sewing on wound stripes."[42]

By January in Andernach, Germany, she came down with the flu: "Yes, at last I'm in style and have had the 'flu' with the rest of the world. Lieut. Brown of the Medical Corps took care of me, and it seemed quite natural to have a Dr. Brown coming in. They all teased me by telling me what a nice military funeral they'd give me, but I fooled them and didn't die after all." Shortly thereafter, she received a cable from her father asking her to return to New Jersey.[43] Officers from the Seventh US Infantry held a going-away party for her on February 24 at Hohenzollern Castle, and after a lengthy trip through France, she sailed for home in March. The scrapbook features of these last months include photos and descriptions of places visited, ephemera from going-away events, and letters of appreciation for her service. One page of her scrapbook covering February 26 to March 11, 1919, includes her photo ID, her service chevron permit, a Red Triangle League membership card in her married name, "Mrs. J. G. Carswell (Emma Dickson)" (after her return from Europe, Dickson married James Graham Carswell), and a clipping of a poem by E. Louise Whiting titled "Let me go back to France":

Let me go back to France!
I'll stifle in this ease
This doing as I please—
Let me go back to France! . . .
They call! They're calling me to come!
But I forget—you cannot hear
The voices ever in my ear!
"I am so tired of war," you say?
Yes, yes—I, too; but so are they—
War-weary are they every one.
But tell them, tell them that I come!
You've not been there—how could you know
The memories that haunt me so!

Emma Dickson's careful construction of the scrapbook in the years following her experiences speak to the strong cultural and social imperative for personal archiving started earlier in diaries and travel narratives but strengthened by portable photography; but in a time of war,

Dickson, like many other Americans, could take tourist tropes only so far in framing her experiences of war abroad. Helen Bagoe and Emma Dickson may have started out by framing their travels as "wonderful experiences" that would lead to self improvement, but the trope soon became that of "walking through a nightmare" of which only the most distant snapshots could be taken, even if the camerist was very close to the trauma. Emma Dickson's scrapbook, with its diversity of materials, its honesty, and its visual silences, exemplifies personal archiving as one method of managing the experience of trauma. In its pages, Dickson could literally place her materials in the national narrative and try to give meaning to the intensity of suffering and death to which she was a witness.

Americans further removed from the dangers of war used their cameras to record the return of their loved ones from abroad. Photos of homecoming events are common in local and state archives in the United States. A series of images of Honor Day homecoming festivities in Richland County, Wisconsin, offer evidence that consumers found the autographic Kodak useful in recording their First World War memory practices, including a photo of a large community "Service Flag." In the United States, communities honored households with members serving in the military during wartime with a flag bearing a single blue star. In 1918, on a recommendation from the Women's Committee of the Council of National Defenses, President Wilson authorized the practice of covering the blue star with a gold one if the family had lost one of its members to the war.[44] The photo from Richland County shows a community version, with those who had lost a family member pinning gold stars to the flag.[45] Likewise, one of Richland's amateur photographers captured the display honoring the dead with a photo inscribed "Flower Pavilion Honor Day, Richland Ctr, Wis. 7-25-1919."[46] Photos of reviewing stands, parading soldiers, street scenes, and so on in the Richland collection include autographic inscriptions that attest to the camera user's awareness of the present as a future historical event.

Ad campaigns that promoted the American consumers' duties as recordkeepers made Kodak very successful during the war. (Its net profits climbed steadily from 1914 to 1920.)[47] The company came out with a line of products that emphasized in particular the importance of archiving war photos, noting that special albums and photo holders were warranted for safeguarding memories (though the ads stopped short of explicitly saying that the materials could be used to memorialize the dead). One advertisement for a special photo album urged consumers to "Keep the Portraits of your Heroes. Give them the care they deserve, securely held in a substantial album." The ad shows a watercolor print of a couple sitting on a couch looking at an album, while the inset features that same couple in their older years, looking at the same album.[48] Kodak was so successful during the war selling cameras, film, and albums that by October 1918 the company was urging limits to the hard sell, telling dealers that in light of materials rationing, they should "discourage the use of photography except in so far as it aids in the successful prosecution of the war" and that "unnecessary snap-shotting should be discouraged."[49]

Janina Struk, in her transnational study of soldiers' photography, *Private Pictures: Soldiers' Inside View of War*, rightly identifies World War I as a turning point in the history of chronicling warfare, a moment when more participants than ever before had access to visual recording technology. Her analysis of national differences in soldiers' photo albums from the First World War, while limited by sample size, offers some intriguing clues about the distinctiveness of American soldiers' understandings of their experiences. She identifies dominant themes by nationality. While Polish soldiers' albums highlighted national pride, those made by German soldiers demonstrated singularity of purpose. The common theme in British soldiers' albums was the imperial gaze, and the dominant theme in photo albums made by American soldiers, she argues, was confusion.[50] While a larger sample size may be needed to confirm these conclusions, identifying confusion as a dominant theme in American albums does seem warranted. Their late entry in the war, their country's geographic distance from the fighting and its consequences, and their primarily economic rather than military contributions to early war efforts could explain American soldiers' confusion about the war's realities. Another explanation could be the dominance of consumer fantasy in American culture. When every storefront, every streetcar, and every newspaper carried the message that the war would present itself as a form of tourism or a grand way to be a part of history, encounters with real violence, inhumane conditions, and illness and injury whether to oneself or to others could reasonably be expected to produce a perplexity not recognized in the dominant public dialogue about photography's role in American society.

When peace was secured, Kodak seamlessly transitioned back to marketing the connection between picture taking and leisure travel or family which had dominated its promotional efforts before the war, but the urgency of memory keeping remained a constant theme. Usually picturing affluent couples or young families in their leisure or travel adventures—skiing, checking into hotels, enjoying the beach, touring about in automobiles capturing the "quaint" and "picturesque"— postwar ads emphasized the role the corporation could play in fulfilling one's duty to record history. This commercial narrative in the postwar years trivialized the trauma of war and rhetorically disallowed full readjustment to civilian life and peace.

Chapter Five

"A VISIBLE TOKEN"

Expanding the Promise of the Kodak
in the Interwar Years

Access to cameras and transportation continued to expand after the First World War, and Kodak capitalized on the opportunities to reach new mobile markets. In the early twentieth century, the Eastman Kodak Company recognized that its profits depended on cultural engagement through advertising, and specifically on privileged Americans' sense of duty to preserve their personal history. The vacations of the growing middle class needed to be recorded for posterity, the logic of the ads went, because this professional and managerial class supported national power; *their* story was the story of the nation. By making its product central to a system of privilege based on class, ethnicity, mobility, and nationality, Kodak claimed a key role in supporting American cultural and economic power. Its marketing fantasies of individual geographic mobility and control over history must be considered in the context of the global system Kodak put in place to facilitate the very fantasies it promoted in its advertising. Annual reports in the first three decades of the twentieth century reflected a commitment to global growth. Kodak built a worldwide infrastructure of retail outlets, wholesale markets, and processing establishments, which by 1930 boasted 244 branches and subsidiaries representing six continents to supply authorized dealers in every country of the world.[1] Reports regularly featured images of Kodak plants, distributors, and wholesale and retail branches far from Rochester. The 1928 report included four pages of images of Kodak facilities in countries outside the United States, including France, Germany, Hungary, China, South Africa, Brazil, and Cuba.[2] Reports in the 1920s included color maps attesting to Kodak's stature as a global corporation, and the 1930 report included a retrospective of the company that explicitly addressed its international ambitions: "The Company's policy from the beginning has been to develop markets for its products in every country of the world. This program has been followed consistently, and not only provides international service to its customers but also stabilizes the business."[3] The death of founder George Eastman in 1932 corresponded with the international economic depression, and profits dropped precipitously after 1930, curtailing the company's global ambitions. Following World War II, earnings and ambitions would eventually recover to pre-depression figures, but the 1930s had provided a reality check.[4]

As the Kodak Company's operations expanded, though, so did Kodak users' experiments with the camera, documenting new ways of travel and thinking about the transformative power of travel for individual and collective identity. The end of the war meant renewed opportunities for European travel, and manufacturing innovation and rising wages put automobiles within reach of more Americans. Increasing mobility in the 1920s occurred at the same time that accelerated cultural experimentation brought about by youth culture, the Harlem Renaissance, the Great Migration, and new ideas about gender as Americans came to terms with the cultural implications of the Nineteenth Amendment. Cameras recorded this cultural experimentation, especially through travel, producing pictures that diverged from Kodak's marketing, which centered the white upper-middle-class woman as the keeper of the family's visual archive and white upper-middle-class family members as the actors. Photos from the 1920s and 1930s—at least the ones that made their way into archives—include subjects engaged in disrupting existing power dynamics and stereotypes: women wearing men's wear and men wearing women's wear; African Americans claiming public spaces; Native Americans using modern technology. In its advertising, Kodak failed to represent the diversity of its market in its ads, viewing its clientele with the same lens it had used since 1888, updating only the cars and the clothes. Such myopia overlooked the expansion of the mass production of memory as a cultural practice and revealed the limits of the corporation's role in the mass practice of personal archiving. While remaining a highly profitable company, Kodak planted the seeds of its own irrelevance in American culture while continuing to innovate in technology.

As some Americans began to question their photographic habits, public dialogue leaned toward justification for the tired tropes of tourist snaps. Gertrude Levy's account of tourist photography in Europe in 1927 framed the relationship between travel and cameras in terms of personal expression through sameness. She wrote, "Of the thousands of our fellow-countrymen abroad each summer, most of them travel with a camera; and nowhere is the American spirit of conformity more strikingly evident" than in the subjects they photographed. Whether Americans pictured the Bridge of Sighs, St. Mark's Basilica, and gondoliers in Venice or William Tell's chapel and "every ruined castle in the Rhineland . . . the results will be as alike as peas in a pod." This predictability, however, was not so predictable after all, for each tourist photographer wanted his or her own photo of historic landscapes and picturesque people, "a visible token of something that he has seen with his own eyes, and recorded with his own hand . . . an attempt to crystallize a memorable emotion, a fusion of himself with the scene."[5] Levy's tourists sought a place to situate themselves temporarily in an imagined past.

Hobbyists writing in *Photo Era Magazine* started to use the term "photographic vacation" or "photographer's holiday" to describe the opportunity of combining their hobby with an established social practice. W. X. Kinchloe advised that "selecting the camera for use on a photographic vacation is the one thing above all others that should not be put off until the last moment."[6] James Basey observed that "during each summer season, thousands of Americans make a trip to Europe, of whom probably ninety percent use photographic apparatus of one sort or another." Among them was the "advanced amateur," one "to whom photography is one of the joys of living, one who has gone into thoroughly, one who has mastered, to a great extent, the technical side of his hobby. One of the great incentives of his trip is the opportunity afforded for the exercise of his hobby."[7] Increasing numbers of tourists pointed lenses at the world's ruins, historic architecture, monuments, and people they considered "quaint" and lost to a modernity based on technological skill. The public dialogue on tourist photography often took on gendered overtones as well. Writing in *Photo Era* in 1928, W. Robert Moore gave advice on getting good shots of women, who "are usually more difficult to photograph, because they are more particular about the appearance than men."[8] The association of travel with the camera seemed complete in this literature; only the nuances needed discussing.

Accounts by travelers with cameras in this period reflected a tourist infrastructure responding to their needs. By 1921, camerist Herbert Turner reported that for a traveler "landing at Marseilles . . . there is a good chance . . . to restock with Eastman goods," and if the tourist found himself away from camera supplies in Europe, all he had to do was send "a telegraph or postcard to the simple address 'Eastman Kodak Company, Paris' asking for photo-supplies to be sent c.o.d. to a given address on his route." If the photographer had to develop his own pictures, "in many hotels in Europe there are darkrooms at the disposition of guests."[9] James Basey's trip to Nice in 1923 included a visit with a local photo finisher, a Mr. Columb, who reported that "a large proportion of his trade is devoted to American tourists." Columb's shop was only one of many photo-finishing firms in Nice, which had a regular contingent of American Kodak customers. Basey also reported that "most Continental hotels have a darkroom for the use of their guests" who weren't taking advantage of the Kodak "you press the button and we do the rest" system.[10] In 1926, photographer Roland Gorbold confirmed Basey's observations by noting that "a camera is found in the baggage of almost every tourist." Gorbold also acknowledged the presence of services available for photographers abroad, dividing his travels into places where such services were available and places where they were not: "It has been my good fortune to wander over a considerable part of the earth's surface, sometimes in places where all the requirements of the photographer can be purchased, and at other times off the beaten track far from the haunts of the Kodak dealer, ubiquitous though he be."[11] Camerist Gertrude Levy remarked that the numbers of American tourists with cameras landing in Europe compared with the numbers of immigrants landing at Ellis Island. Like Basey, Levy reported talks with a European photo finisher, this one a Mr. Lucien Rode of Paris, who "averages one hundred and fifty rolls [processed] per day" for American tourists. Rode told her that "the American tourist makes the best photographs in the world. . . . And the reason is, he uses a fool-proof camera."[12] The Kodak, even in the hands of American fools, could turn out a good picture.

Aggressive or subversive tactics used by some tourist photographers seem to have been taken as a matter of course in the amateur photography literature by 1930. John McFarlane, in a 1930 article titled "Permettez! Camera Adventures in Europe," advised American tourist photographers that the "Western motto holds good: 'Shoot first and ask afterwards!' While hidden from the victim, the camera is set, the right moment arrives, and—snap!" In addition to wielding the camera like a concealed weapon, the touring camerist could simply project authority: "Another way is to be rather officious. It is strange, but most people will obey anyone who seems to have authority."[13] McFarlane's article endorsed the belief of Americans that they had a right to freely photograph the world, whether the world wanted to be photographed or not, because it had been left behind by modernity. This attitude developed in the context of the growth of the American upper middle class and the increase in American economic and political influence in the first few decades of the twentieth century, and the camera had become a prop to represent American progress and power. Americans with cameras pictured landscapes and people they considered left over from the past while placing themselves squarely in a position of power in the present.

A new wave of automobility inspired Americans to travel at home, particularly African Americans looking for a way around the Jim Crow restrictions of the rail system, women seeking release from domestic containment, Native Americans exercising their rights to mobility in the face of the reservation system, and growing LGBTQ communities looking for freedom from the stresses of heteronormativity. In the period following World War I, Americans not pictured in "Take a Kodak with you" advertising took up cameras anyway, documenting their mobility and offering visual evidence of worlds outside the stereotypes. Their travels often looked different from those journeys taken by wealthier, white heterosexual couples, and economics played a crucial role in shaping one's vacations. Working-class and lower-middle-class people chose vacations that fit easily into their work, such as sightseeing on a work trip or doing one's work at a vacation destination, and they took shorter vacations than people of means. Budget-conscious tourists chose automobile camping or boardinghouses over the pricier resort hotels.[14] Wealthier people of color and Jewish people found themselves iced out of the posh hotels even when they could afford the stay, and resorts organized for people of color, LBGTQ communities, and religious minorities formed to meet the demand created by the discriminatory practices of the service industry.[15] Public transportation remained in the clutches of de jure segregation in the South and de facto segregation in the North, a condition African Americans fought tenaciously.[16] These conditions led to differences in the vacation photos produced. Compared to those kept by more privileged tourists, the albums of people not pictured in the dominant culture's images of tourists placed more emphasis on shots privileging family and community and fewer "ethnographic," imperial gaze photos and architectural landscape shots. The inclusion of automobiles emphasized individualized mobility, and the common theme of beach snapshots emphasized the centrality of seaside and lakeside recreation in the expansion of vacations. Mass travel and mass photography provided an opportunity to edit bigotry out of the frame and to narrow the focus on community and individuality.

In the first two decades of the twentieth century, cars came within reach of more and more Americans, and the freedom of driving resonated particularly with African Americans. Automobile ownership rose from eight thousand in 1900 to 23.1 million in 1929, and in that time, the car in the popular imagination went from being a rich man's toy to a marker of citizenship. Significantly, Americans associated the automobile with freedom and self-determination.[17] For African Americans, the open road had additional appeal. White privilege fully informed the infrastructure of railroad tourism, for depots and railcars offered ample opportunity for the sorting of passengers into racial categories. As the travel historian Kathleen Franz demonstrates, in the early years of automobility, many African Americans saw the automobile as a tool for undermining the apartheid of railroad travel; as one Black driver noted, "It's good for the spirit to just give the old railroad Jim Crow the laugh."[18] Motoring, though, could be a dangerous form of enjoyment. African American accounts of road travel in this period abound with records of threats, violence, harassment, and humiliation. Black motorists encountered numerous and diverse difficulties in finding food and lodging, and developed coping strategies that included making detailed prearrangements to stay with friends and being quick to recognize danger and coordinate a response.[19] By 1936, African American travelers had another option for managing automobile travel: Victor Green's handbook *The Negro Traveler's Green Book*, a publication produced yearly to facilitate Black motorists' travel by listing places to find lodging, food, and other services. The resource offered help in all corners of the United States; in 1956, it listed sixteen hotels and restaurants in Kansas City and seventeen in Buffalo.[20] Such mechanisms demonstrated African American motorists' commitment to the idea that driving represented self-determination.

Like automobiles, cameras offered African Americans a method of asserting control in a racist society committed to the perpetuation of images meant to ridicule Blacks.[21] Those pictures available in public archives reveal three types of photos and photo arrangements that related to tourism and mobility: beach photos, photos of people with cars, and photos of family and friends on holiday.

Surf recreation in the early and mid-twentieth century created and cemented ties of family and friendship, and the camera played a central role in the recording and remembering of times spent at the beach. Cadaine Hairston of East Rutherford, New Jersey, kept an album throughout the 1920s that documented her beach-going activities. Her photos include shots of visits to Keansburg Beach, Rockaway Beach, and Asbury Park, all within a day's travel from her home. She took photos of swimmers posing at the shoreline, hanging onto ropes in the surf, and lounging in the sand, and arranged the photos by trip, providing captions on the album and on the photos themselves. These commented on the relationships among individuals pictured. On a 1927 trip to the beach, Grace Atwater took time out of the surf to pose for Hairston's camera wearing her bathing attire and holding what looks like a stuffed animal, possibly won in a boardwalk game. Hairston made sure to point out one key feature of the photo with the caption "Showing her ring. Step aside boys." In 1924 the young woman documented her trip to Keansburg Beach, showing couples and groups enjoying the outdoors and one another's company. In this set of photos, she placed a small picture of herself in the midst of playfully captioned photos of friends (figure 13).

Hairston's album went beyond bathing suit shots, however, and included multiple photos of couples and friends posing elegantly on the beach in fashionable eveningwear. An album from Mary Woods covering 1918 to 1922 featured individuals, couples, and groups enjoying themselves at the beach, but in this case the participants came in colder weather and posed in their wool coats. Like Cadaine Hairston, Mary Woods captioned her photos to record who was in them and, sometimes, the place where the photo was taken. A few photos are captioned with both, such as the youthful, smiling group of thirteen excursionists she labeled "The Yorktown Bunch."[22]

Figure 13. Page from an album belonging to Cadaine Hairston documenting a trip to Keansburg Beach in New Jersey in 1924. Note the centrality of the album's creator surrounded by friends and family. Robert Langmuir African American Photograph Collection, Stuart A. Rose Manuscript, Archives, and Rare Book Library, Emory University.

The Hairston and Woods beach photos and album arrangements should be seen in the context of changing conditions for African Americans' participation in shore leisure in the 1920s and 1930s. The leisure historian Victoria Wolcott demonstrates that beaches before 1920, particularly in the North, were likely to be integrated, although instances of beach segregation grew along with popularity of beach resorts in the latter half of the nineteenth century. The Asbury Park beach that Cadaine Hairston photographed had been segregated since the 1880s, when the leader of a Methodist summer camp led a movement to exclude African Americans from the waterfront. After the Great Migration, both northern and southern cities made attempts to limit Black access to water recreation.[23] This had different effects for different classes of African Americans. Wealthier African Americans, working with land developers, created Black resort areas with privately owned cottages, like Highland Beach in Maryland. For lower-class African Americans living in cities, the segregation meant taking their chances in remote, polluted, and unsafe swimming areas, which led to large numbers of drowning deaths, particularly among Black youth. As Andrew W. Kahrl found in his study of African American beaches in the early twentieth century, possession of swimming skills became a marker of higher class status because it took a measure of wealth and influence to access the safe waters required to build such skills.[24] Photographs and album arrangements centered on beach leisure, then, were tangible reminders of success and status.

Another common image found in early twentieth-century albums arranged by both whites and African Americans was the automobile pose: individuals, couples, and groups had their photos taken in, next to, and on automobiles. Some cars were new and shiny, while others appear very well used. The William A. Clement Collection at the University of North Carolina at Chapel Hill contains a set of photos clipped from an album put together in the 1920s or 1930s. Clement, a businessman from Durham, lived from 1912 to 2001, and the photos were probably collected from his relatives and taken during his youth. Although the captions were lost to the clipping, the contents reveal a family taking up the popular consumer technologies of the day: cameras and cars. While some photos appear to have been taken on occasions when the subjects had purchased a new car, others appear to record a pause during travel. As with car photos in other albums created by African Americans, the car does not appear alone in the Clement album. It was not simply a consumer product to display but instead a feature of life in families and communities; the albums present the cars as a technology for maintaining ties among people. One album dating from around 1920, whose provenance has been lost, features a couple on their travels to the waterfront, to unique architectural features, and to a tropical or subtropical location. The couple made the trips together, for the images feature either the man or the woman posing, but not both; clearly the other one was taking the photo. Interspersed with photos showing them posed with palm trees, buildings, and a waterfront is a beautifully framed shot of a woman with her foot on the running board of the car amid plants in the foreground on either side. While it is indeed a posed photo, the pose, with the door open, the woman's body almost in the car, and her hand lightly on the doorframe, indicates that the subject felt a great deal of comfort with the technology; the pose shows the automobile as a rather natural extension of the photo's subject.[25] The regular appearance of automobile photos in the albums is not surprising, given the cultural emphasis on driving and the increased availability of cars after 1908. Like the beach photos, the car photos serve as tangible reminders of mobility, success, and self-determination.

While album creators often featured beaches and cars, these themes were both part of a larger commitment to the subject of family and community during times of leisure. With the exception of photos of mothers taking care of babies, the albums captured very little work through the lens, making the camera an instrument with which to shape an identity through leisure. Mary Woods, Cadaine Hairston, and the snapshotters whose names have been lost produced albums whose purpose was to document ties among people. One later album included a World War II–era set of photos captioned "Lester and Valerie," showing a man in uniform holding a baby, one photo featuring a pose in a garden, while in another he is next to a monument to Booker T. Washington.[26] Mary Woods arranged photos in a series labeled "In Smithfield, PA, 1918" that pictured couples and groups consistently captioned with their names or their relationships to one another like "Real Pals" or "Old Sweethearts."[27] Cadaine Hairston included multiple photos of the same outdoor ornamental pump house, but each one shows different people, sometimes individuals and sometimes couples.

The 1940–41 album "Seattle" demonstrates the increasing availability of both cameras and cars and users' management of the image of both in albums produced by African Americans. This album features a road trip to the Pacific Northwest that highlights the waterfront, walking tours, ferry transport, driving, and even a photo of a hotel, but all include at least one person. (The main subject of the photo with the hotel in the background is a man checking the bill. The creator captioned it "The Days Receipt.") The album's creator seems to have been focused on documenting all of the features of the trip but, more important, all of the people who took part in it, for he or she captioned each photo with a reference to the trip: "Looking in on China Town," "Over the sea," or, above one picture of a couple with the woman sitting on the curb and the man standing behind her, "He walked her to death."[28] The album's creator fashioned an image of a busy group on holiday, including a photo of a man posing with his foot on the front bumper of an automobile on the open road with the caption "Off for a little rest." The album documents very little rest, however, but instead features a great deal of movement, activity, and social interaction. In their albums, Mary Woods, Cadaine Hairston, and the maker of "Seattle" included mainly photos that focus on people; in contrast to a survey of the George Eastman House archives of travel albums made by wealthier white people, the albums made by African American camerists reveal much less landscape and architecture as central subject matter. While photos of tourists on holiday abound in the Eastman House albums, so do those of ruins, architecture, and landscape, as well as "foreign" people. Very few of the albums created by African American vacationers included these themes, likely because public space was much more dangerous for African American tourists than it was for whites. Instead the lenses of Black travelers focused on their families and friends, documenting their presence in new and novel settings. While many white camerists chose to take photos of historic landscapes, monuments, and architecture in an attempt to record the past before its inevitable capitulation to modernity, Black traveler-photographers chose to highlight their own communities, families, and friends in an effort to record and relay their stories from their own perspectives.[29]

African American travel photography in the early twentieth century is important to understanding the connections among technology, historical agency, and the growth of the leisure economy in the early twentieth century. African American travelers operated their cameras as mnemonic devices to construct and control their histories and memories. As witness to their mobility and leisure time, the camera played a significant role in crafting a reality apart from the more vicious and dangerous realities posed by white violence and racism. Certainly African American vacationers faced discrimination and threats when traveling, but in their own leisure economy, they bonded with one another and enjoyed some relief from work and the stresses of living in a racist society. The combination of automobile leisure travel and amateur camera use provided useful ways for making space away from the restrictions of Jim Crow. As they worked to dismantle the Jim Crow system, they used the camera to document their travels and present an image of life free from the problems of segregation. Middle-class African Americans' adoption of automobility and mass photography needs to be seen in the context of community building, just as historians have seen Black communities' efforts to build churches, schools, and access to the ballot.

Cadaine Hairston, Mary Woods, and other African American travelers were not alone in eschewing the imperial gaze in favor of highlighting family and personal experience. Adelheid Zeller, a twenty-nine-year-old schoolteacher from Scranton, Pennsylvania, had linguistic and recent ancestral ties to Europe when she traveled there in 1922. Her father, the Reverend Paul E. Zeller, had been born in Indiana to German parents, while her mother, Marie, was a first-generation immigrant from Germany. In 1920, Reverend Zeller was pastor at Scranton's Church of Peace, while Adelheid's sisters, both in their twenties, worked as schoolteachers as well. The census lists German as each parent's "native tongue."[30] Adelheid's trip from January 24 to August 26, 1922, was breathtakingly busy. She took in Paris, London, Munich, Rome, Milan, Cologne, and Lucerne, making long lists of buildings visited in her diary and describing architectural and design details. Her letters home added more details: what she ate, the look of taxis, how many steps she took walking up to a cathedral, how flowers were displayed at the market, the compliments she received on her German and her growing proficiency in French.

Her photo album matched the energy of the trip. When she returned, she produced a captionless album with photos crowded onto every page (378 photos survived in her album at the time it was archived in the early 1970s). Zeller's album is similar to Grace Franklin's from nearly twenty years earlier, but in addition to having no captions, it is also more densely packed with photos. Zeller and her party took many different types of shots: people on the street, architectural details and wide angles, travel party snapshots, landscape views. Zeller was particularly fascinated by architecture, and she made sure to include ample documentation of the buildings, their surroundings, and their features. She recorded many famous sites, such as the Milan Cathedral, the Leaning Tower of Pisa, ruins of the Roman Forum (including some shots very similar to those taken by the Wheelers in 1900–1901), Big Ben, and the Lion of Lucerne, framing the shots carefully, almost reverentially.[31] Unlike some American tourists abroad, Zeller and her party did not pose for photos while climbing on or standing in historic buildings or ruins. When the Zeller party took pictures of themselves, they were in the street, on a rock, in a streetcar, on a ship, on a bench. As the child of a minister, Zeller may have been used to having her public behavior monitored closely. As a person with relatives living in Europe, she may have been more aware of European views of her as an American. Having lived through her twenties during the First World War as a person with German immigrant parents and grandparents, she may have developed a cautiousness with regard to her public behavior. Whereas Zeller visited the metropoles of Europe, some of the photos of tourists climbing on ruins were taken by those visiting current or former colonies of Britain and Spain, which could have made them feel freer to impose their meanings visually with their bodies dominating the landscape. Her keen attention to detail could also have shaped Zeller's relationship to the public spaces in which she took her photos. Zeller clearly showed propensities toward memory work with her detailed journal and copious photographic collection of her trip. She was just, quite simply, serious about learning the history of the places she went. At some point in her thirties or early forties, she married Ilbert Lacy, a sanitary engineer, and together they took up local history, eventually producing a study of Lockport, New York, newspapers for the Niagara County Historical Society.[32]

For any number of reasons, Adelheid Zeller produced photos that demonstrate more circumspect behavior in public spaces than that of many tourists, but she was not alone. The exigencies of navigating public space informed the vacation photos of individuals who by appearance or behavior departed from dominant norms of gender. In the middle of the nineteenth century, the sex segregation of middle-class culture and society accommodated romantic affection between those of the same sex, as letters and diary entries attest, while historical sources like wills and other official documents evidence lifelong same-sex commitments in this period.[33] Historians of sexuality identify the late nineteenth and early twentieth centuries as a period of significant changes in thinking about sexuality. Broadening acceptance and use of birth control provided some separation of sexuality from its procreative function, while the growing consumer economy emphasized individual pleasure. The concepts of heterosexuality and homosexuality—which tied identity to sexual behaviors—emerged in this period, and communities of people sharing similar sexual identities began to grow as a presence in cities. Individuals in these communities nevertheless faced social stigma and sometimes violence when negotiating public spaces outside their communities.[34] The solidification of sexual identity with heterosexuality as normative over the first few decades of the twentieth century informed vernacular photography by those identifying and identified as homosexual. Tourist photography could be tricky, for in the common spaces of tourism and for the sake of safety, one would have to be guarded in behaviors exhibited with one's travel partner. But at the same time, vacation—even in heteronormative communities—could provide a space in which to experiment with gender norms. As Cindy Aron demonstrated in *Working at Play*, vacations afforded opportunities for some women to test restrictions on their movement and gender roles even as other vacation practices reinforced gender, class, and racial prescriptions. At resorts, women tried sports, competition with men, risqué dress, and other behaviors that were not a part of their non-resort life.[35]

Stigma attached to same-sex love affected historical memory by limiting photography in two ways. First, for the most part because of limitations in the technology, most amateur photos had to be taken outside, in the full light of day—which was not always safe for sexual minorities facing the threat not just of stigma but also of criminal charges. Depending on the space, self-censorship may have been a requirement. Second, relatives often destroyed historical evidence of same-sex relationships after the passing of their "inverted" kin.[36] Despite these challenges— and they were quite powerful ones—a photographic record of same-sex affection and experimentation with dominant gendered forms has survived, some of it documenting leisure travel and recreation. In her study of the early twentieth-century celebrity female impersonator Julian Eltinge, Sharon R. Ullman documented experimental gender presentation and its perceived relationship to sexual practice in an age she describes as a "period of intense gender anxiety." Ullman shows that Eltinge and other male performers of femininity on paid entertainment circuits used photography to demonstrate the relationship between their female stage personae and their masculinity and implied sexual preferences. One reviewer praised Eltinge's minstrel show in terms of the camera itself: "Just as a white man makes the best stage Negro, so a man gives a more photographic interpretation of femininity than the average woman is able to give." Eltinge's celebrity rested on his "performance" offstage as a masculine, heterosexual man, for as Ullman notes, he was "a notorious camera hound, [and] most photos of Eltinge pointedly depicted him out of female attire." As Ullman's study shows, however, men whose affections for other men had to stay hidden could use photography as a witness to their own identities, for police raids turned up private photos of gender experimentation, such as in the case of a man in Long Beach, California, who "carried a photograph of himself dressed in a gorgeous frock and a plumed hat sniffing flowers in front of his bungalow."[37] Even when confronted by crime photographers, some of these gender innovators embraced the opportunity provided by the camera to perform, such as in the photojournalist Weegee's image of a man in women's clothing emerging from a police vehicle smiling and lifting his skirt to reveal a shapely leg.[38] As I noted in chapter 2, Alice Austen made early use of the camera to imagine gender and implied sexual preferences differently. Travel snapshots by people in the process of shaping modern LGBTQ identities showed an awareness of the camera's potential for identity formation and community building.

The Canadian history scholar Linda L. Revie provides insight on the limits and possibilities of experimentation with photography and gender in her case study of Ella Liscombe, an unmarried lower-middle-class woman whose personal archive clearly demonstrates a use of vacation as an opportunity to play with gendered forms. On one excursion in particular, a 1927 "Adamless Eden" camping trip to Cape Breton Island, Liscombe and her female companions chose to wear men's clothing for the whole time, slept together in one large tent, and developed coded language to describe their activities. Photographs that show them at rest from fishing, swimming, or preparing camp while in male clothing offer evidence of the consciousness of experiment. In describing a photo of their discarded feminine clothing hanging on trees, Revie notes that "one can hardly miss the sartorial suggestiveness." Liscombe and her companions, however, returned to feminine clothing at the conclusion of the vacation, which indicated a "remarkable combination of self-invention and self-knowledge."[39]

The same could be said of Pauli Murray's photo album titled "The 'Life and Times' of an American called Pauli Murray," which included photos documenting the early life and education of the writer, activist, lawyer, and minister. Before graduation from Howard Law School in 1944 and subsequent career as a notable civil rights jurist and first woman of color to be ordained as an Episcopal priest, Pauli Murray fought for—and gained—their education, wrote poetry and prose, organized for workers and workers' rights, protested segregation on buses, and experimented with gender identity. They researched and wrote family history and autobiography and were, in the words of Murray's biographer Rosalind Rosenberg, "a pack rat," bequeathing "to the Schlesinger Library at Radcliffe College at Harvard University more than 135 boxes of diaries, interviews, scrapbooks, organizational minutes, papers, speeches, articles, poems, sermons, medical records, pictures, audiotapes, books, and letters (those received as well as copies of those sent)."[40] Murray saw the importance of personal archiving, as Rosenberg notes, to the fulfillment of a familial destiny to make a difference. "The 'Life and Times' of an American called Pauli Murray" showed a young person using education and travel to find the sense of self that would equip and fortify them for the work of meeting those high expectations. In their travels, and travel photography, they tried out selves.

Pauli Murray's photo album, while covering the years between 1919 and 1951, concentrates most heavily on travels in the 1930s, a time when they lived in New York going to Hunter College, working various jobs, and seeking out experience in advocating for workers. They circulated in the socially, culturally, and politically vibrant world of the Harlem Renaissance and engaged in activist and literary work. While the earlier photos in their seventy-two-page album focus on family in North Carolina and Maryland and schooling at Hillside High School in Durham, the photos from the early 1930s show a Murray recognizing many different parts of their adult life. Although the photos of school life in Durham usually show Murray in dresses (even though they often wore boys' clothing), they appear mostly in more masculine attire in the pages featuring what Murray termed "many moods and facets of my 'id.'" The page includes "The Bust," a sculpture of Murray by Maysie Stone; "The Poet, Central Park, N.Y.C.," showing Murray in jodhpurs and jacket, looking down at the photographer; "The Imp," a head-and-shoulders shot of Murray smiling; and "The Acrobat, Durham, N.C. 1931," showing Murray in an impressive backbend. "The Crusader" portrays them in a dress and coat, ready for activist work, while the photo labeled "The Dude 1931" features Murray in masculine attire and haircut, sitting confidently on a stone wall. Among these, "The Vagabond, Bridgeport, Conn. 1931" is most illustrative of Murray's use of travel photography to depict geographic mobility as an opportunity to experiment socially and culturally. "The Vagabond" was taken during a hitchhiking trip to Connecticut with a friend, Dorothy Hayden, when the two dressed as Boy Scouts and got rides where they could. As Rosenberg relates the story, Hayden and Murray were caught "disguised" as men in Bridgeport. In the photo, Murray sits on a stone monument with one leg raised, dressed in boots, pants, jacket, high wool socks, and hat, short hair sticking out from under it. This Boy Scout look is one Murray commonly used in travel throughout the thirties as they regularly took to the roads, rails, and even to the sky in one instance. In the spring of 1931, Murray hitchhiked to California and, upon learning of an aunt's illness, hopped freight cars to return to Durham. These daring travels provided inspiration for literary output, resulting in the poem "The Song of the Highway" and "Three Thousand Miles on a Dime in Ten Days," both published in the famous *Negro: An Anthology* in 1934.[41] Like the literary works, Murray's snapshots attested to love of movement. Out of doors, on the move, and dressed more comfortably in masculine clothing, they photographed the places and people that intrigued them, including companions, who in turn photographed Murray. They used a wide variety of shots, as if everything on the road was interesting, attending to photography as best they could on a limited budget. A page in the photo album titled "San Francisco May 1931" includes three shots of the bay accompanied by a bracketed note: "[These shots were taken with an ancient second hand Kodak purchased in a Chinese shop for 50 cents]." Murray created a scrapbook of these experiences titled "Vagabondia."[42]

More than half of Pauli Murray's 1919–51 photograph album is devoted to travel. Despite working a variety of jobs, facing persistent food insecurity and a lack of funds, Murray graduated from Hunter College in 1933. Trips to Connecticut and California during college inspired additional wandering, this time with Peggie Holmes, whom the Murray scholar Patricia Bell-Scott describes as "a round-faced, golden haired camp counselor from an upper-class family in Putnam County, New York. She was athletic, fun-loving, and popular...nicknamed 'the second Babe Ruth.'"[43] In the mid-thirties Murray traveled often with Holmes: camping, auto touring, riding freight cars. The album contains a number of photos taken with Holmes, including four pages of snapshots of Murray and Holmes camping titled "The Days of Camping and Beachcombing 193[?]–1937 'Bayberry Island' on Reynolds Channel between Long Beach Far Rockaway, L.I." They photographed their camp, each other, and fellow campers, island views, and a couple of unusual shots, one of a fellow camper sunbathing in the nude and another titled "Pauli Hands and Trees," showing Murray's arms in front of a line of small tree trunks. The collection has a domestic, artsy sensibility, attesting to both intimacy and social experiment. The series "Memories of Newport, R.I." shows hiking exploits—including one of two steep cliffs and the caption "I climbed down to the bottom once at low tide" and two separate but matching photos of Murray and Holmes standing at the top of a rock, wearing identical outfits. These outfits appear again in backyard photos attesting to a social visit, including one of "Pauli and Peggie in an acrobatic stunt" and "An armful," a shot of Pauli carrying Peggie.[44] The two traveled together in the mid-1930s until, ultimately, Holmes could not reconcile with Murray's gender identity, their belief that they were really a man, despite having been assigned female at birth.[45]

Photos taken in the latter half of the 1930s document Murray's marked independence. They put themselves out on the landscape to capture scenes including roads (a favorite topic), water, trees, houses, churches, dunes, mountains, rivers, lakes, and boats. Other snapshots focus on transportation, with one set showing an "Aerial View of White Mountains from a plane" in the summer of 1938. They paid particular photographic attention to "'Susie' the car that cost $25.00 and traveled 2,000 miles without any car trouble—also carried 32 hitchhikers." They captured the car on the street, stuck in sand, and getting pushed to a gas station by hitchhikers. Three document Murray and a stranger tending to mechanical issues: "taking off the spare, while Hitchhiker No. 32 changes the wheel."[46] Beyond the photo of Murray as "Crusader," the album rarely indicates work as an activist, making no mention of Murray's nationally known efforts to desegregate the University of North Carolina or work as a field representative for the National Urban League or with the Workers' Education Project. From Murray's album, few could surmise her participation in classes at the New York Workers School.[47] Their travel photos in the 1930s are open-hearted, grand, experimental—downright Whitmanesque in scope—which makes the page marked "March–May 1940" all the more striking. The page includes two photos of Petersburg Prison in Virginia and two of a courthouse, which Murray explains in a long caption: "Petersburg Prison where I spent Easter Sunday, 1940 after having been arrested for contesting segregation law of Va. on Greyhound interstate bus. Later, after losing appeal of conviction, refused to pay fine and spent 6 days here./This prison was used for Civil War prisoners in 1863–65./Hastings County Courthouse where the trial was held." Murray and friend Adelene McBean, on a trip from New York to Durham, had refused to move when told to take seats farther back on their bus, which resulted in their arrest and imprisonment. The two encountered inhumane prison conditions and much uncertainty over their fate.[48] It was an experience that solidified Murray's already strong commitment to using the law to combat discrimination. They demonstrate frustration in the snapshots; Murray, whose vacation shots show them to be perfectly capable of composing images of buildings and landscapes, took photos of the jail and courthouse that were unbalanced, crooked, and, somehow, just off.[49]

Murray was not the only famous gender innovator to pick up a camera. Gertrude Stein is much better known for her contributions to literary modernism than for her tourist photos, and even conceiving of

Figure 14. Gertrude Stein and Alice B. Toklas pose for a studio portrait
at Aix-les-Bains. Estate of Gertrude Stein and Alice Toklas.
Beinecke Library, Yale University.

Stein as a "tourist" is complicated, for she was born an American and remained so by citizenship but spent most of her adult life in France. A return trip to her native land after thirty years away resulted in the 1937 *Everybody's Autobiography*, part homecoming narrative, part travel narrative, which meditates not only on space but also on change over time.[50] Stein and her life partner, Alice B. Toklas, also traveled quite a bit around France, taking their own photographs and being photographed by their many friends. They took clichéd tourist shots, but they also posed with a seriousness very uncharacteristic of tourist photos. Toklas often casts a deadpan look at the camera, while Stein's face shows an expression of impatience, poses very unlike the warm and humorous snapshots taken in or near their home. Five photograph albums survived among their papers to attest to the couple's travels, home life, and visitors as well as to their archival activities.[51]

The shots from their earliest days in France show them touring a few iconic places in Europe, including the Luxembourg Gardens and the Piazza San Marco, where they took photos in places common to tourists from the days of the Grand Tour. One 1907 shot of Stein has her casually leaning on a railing in Luxembourg Gardens with the statue of the fearless seventeenth-century royal Anne-Marie-Louise d'Orléans in the background.[52] Stein and Toklas posed "in a piazza with pigeons" at Piazza San Marco in Venice around 1908, a pose that had been a cliché promoted by travel books throughout the nineteenth century. As with most clichés, however, Stein and Toklas found them tiresome, for the photo shows the skepticism in their expressions. Toklas stares straight at the camera, unsmiling, while Stein holds two pigeons in her hands, looking unsure about the birds, the camera, or both. Later photos, including those taken on automobile trips, on picnics, and on walks with their dogs Basket and Byron in the Luxembourg Gardens, are similar to other tourist shots, but they differ in the fame of their traveling companions. Painter and costume designer Pavel Tchelitchew traveled with the couple, taking time to pose for a snapshot in their travel clothes, a pause from a picnic. All three subjects, Tchelitchew in the center sitting upright, Toklas at the right sitting up straight with her forearms crossed, and Toklas leaning toward the center from the left, looking impatient for the shutter to complete its task. When the couple visited Aix-les-Bains, a French spa resort town, they posed in a studio with one of the painted backdrops styled in the tradition of a Batoni portrait, complete with the arch of classical architecture. Toklas, in stylish flowered traveling clothes and carrying an ornamented purse, looks out from under a wide-brimmed hat direct-ly at the camera, while Stein, in a rumpled duster, bow tie, and small-brimmed hat, gazes straight at the camera with just the hint of an ironic smile. The studio pose and backdrop appear typical, but the presence of two female subjects in the foreground hints at their relationship, one in the clothing of an eccentric lady, the other in garb evocative of an eccen-tric gentleman, turned slightly toward each other, their elbows close to touching, deep in the center of the image (figure 14).[53]

Two concluding examples from the mass production of memory illus-trate the extent to which Americans used the camera to connect their individual experiences to the longer arc of history as well as the pro-found ways that social position informed the conditions of both photog-raphy and travel. In 1936 Charles, Louise, Nancy, Jean, and Teppy Holton, a white family of German descent from Newark, New Jersey, made wealthy from the pharmaceutical industry, produced a four-volume photo album of their trip to England and Sweden. About two years lat-er, the African American beautician Lida Broner returned to her home in Newark from a nine-month trip to South Africa, bringing her diary, items representing the material culture of South Africa, programs, mag-azines, and enough snapshots for two albums. These citizens of Newark shared a sense that their travels had the potential for instruction, that sharing with others could teach them about the world. Both parties re-corded their trips diligently and took great care in sharing these mate-rials. Both sets of archives eventually made their way to institutions keeping the historical records of Newark: the Holtons' to the Charles F. Cummings New Jersey Information Center at the Newark Public Library and Broner's to the Newark Museum. While the two collections share these characteristics, the differences between them are profound, as were the differences in the conditions that shaped them.

Lida Broner was born in 1895 in Raleigh, North Carolina. In the ear-ly 1900s she moved with her family to New Jersey, where she graduat-ed from high school and took work as a housekeeper and a beautician. Her fascination with the world outside Newark gained expression in her founding of the Women's International Affairs Club, which led her to Max Yergan, a former YMCA missionary and Black activist also born in Raleigh about the same time as Broner.[54] Her connections as an ac-tivist led her to Davidson Don Tengu Jabavu, a South African educator, politician, and preacher who, according to his biographer, "fit very well the model of the 'New African,' able to function in two worlds without apparent conflict."[55] In 1938 Broner took a trip to South Africa by way of London. Jabavu helped her plan the trip and connected her with teachers and community leaders whom she met during her journey throughout South Africa, who supported her travels, invited her to speak, and provided customer referrals as she continued her work as a beautician and Apex Beauty consultant. (Her diary references her work doing hair as well as selling beauty products for that company.) Broner's work as a beautician fit into a larger pattern of Black women's activism through cosmetology, as explored by the historian Tiffany M. Gill, whose work identifies both the beauty shop and the beauty industry as important sites of African American political development and action.[56]

Broner's photos from her trip are only a part of her rich archiving and collecting activities, which included gathering art, clothing, and other items of material culture, as well as news clippings, programs, and ephemera, and creating a detailed travel diary which she later copied by hand. She would go on to create exhibits and educational programs based on this material.[57] The materials she produced about the trip reflected her archival priorities. Her first priority was textual; she kept her diary religiously, recording whom she met, what she did, incidents reflecting the racism that deeply shaped the travel industry, social engagements, speaking engagements, customers served, descriptions of people and places, reflections on power relations, and notes on her own feelings. She shared her joy at the chance to experience "Africa, the land of my forefathers." Her diary includes references to taking "snaps," going to the drugstore to pick up film or prints, and one mention of technical troubles with her camera.[58] She attended to copying her diary right away, focusing on it during her return journey. When her shipmates wanted to talk racial politics, she apparently became frustrated by the time this took, for on January 12 she wrote: "Gee Whiz!! I wish these white folks would stop talking to me. I want to get my diary re-written. Had a dozen interruptions!" Her second archival priority emerged from a sense of the power of education in improving the lives of both Black South Africans and African Americans: collecting. As the curator and Broner biographer Christa Clarke notes, "Broner's collection, encompassing traditional forms of beadwork and pottery as well as art forms taught in mission schools, is emblematic of the opposing emphases on tradition, on the one hand—meaning pride in heritage—and modernity, on the other— the 'new African' in the form of the educated Christian." Upon returning to the United States, Broner became a tireless educator about South Africa, creating exhibits and educational programs and providing information to the media. Her collection was shown at the Newark Museum, the Newark Public Library, the Brooklyn Urban League, and the New York Public Library. According to Clarke, Broner's collection reflected not just a political moment but also personal relationships.[59]

Lida Broner seemed to see photography as an archival activity that had less power than writing and collecting, but the two albums she made about the trip reflected the tone of the other archival activities: the importance of personal relationships in political change and vice versa. Unlike many tourist albums that provide a record of what the tourist saw, Broner's albums record the people she met—teachers, students, families, children, community leaders—and the institutions that hosted her talks and receptions, including community centers, schools, hospitals. They also reflected events, like sailing into Madeira, a reception, and a wedding. Broner's "snaps" were far from spontaneous; individuals pose, smile, and look straight at the camera, indicating that Broner asked permission and posed her subjects. While her ostensible reason for visiting South Africa was to "study the conditions of the Negro" in that country, her photo album has more of the sensibility of a family album: she names people, the subjects look warmly at the photographer, and she arranges photos according to people or events.[60] She created special pages for close friends like Jabavu and Queen Lumkwana, a teacher for students with visual impairments and sometime travel companion. In some ways, Broner used photography to re-create family ties disrupted by diaspora as a tool for homecoming.[61] As she prepared to return to the United States, she wrote in her diary: "My heart is very heavy for I must leave Africa, the land of my forefathers.... We put out to sea at 4PM. Africa! Africa! Africa! The land of my forefathers! I leave Africa with much deeper regret than I left America, my native land. But I will return some day!"[62] Broner's familial feeling of connection with place started before her trip, strengthened during the journey, and lasted a lifetime; the trip led to increased work by Broner on behalf of racial equality and cultural understanding on both sides of the ocean, as she used her experiences and the objects she gathered as exhibition and programming resources.

Around the time Lida Broner left for Africa, fellow New Jerseyite and wealthy white pharmaceutical retiree and local politician Charles W. Holton booked a trip to England and Sweden for his family, a party of five, through Charles Ashmun, a Fifth Avenue travel agent.[63] After their return in the summer of 1936, the Holtons produced a lavish four-volume set of albums that included photographs, hand-drawn maps, detailed itineraries including sites visited and restaurants that served their meals, and a narrative. Each member of the family had a responsibility in the creation of the archive, as listed in volume one: "Mother" wrote the narrative; Bob provided title pages and maps, while Nan and Jean worked on captions. "Father," Nan, Jean, and Teppy took the photos. The collection was hand bound in leather with gold trim, and each volume was stored in its own custom-made box. Photos, rather than being affixed to the pages with photo corners, tape, or paste, were printed on the pages themselves before binding. The Holtons were practiced at both travel and its archiving, and "Mother" started the narrative—in jaunty verse—by framing the current trip in the history of the family's travels since 1933, referencing family trips in 1934 and 1935: "And what you see within this book / Will mark the pleasant path they took." She continued the narrative by connecting their travel to the source of their wealth: "So far the combined drug-manufacturing-selling background of the Dohme-Holton tribe has produced no real cure for that persistent ailment known as 'the itching foot.'" The Holtons' experiences aboard ship, unlike those of Lida Broner, who had to insist on being seated in the dining room and whom other passengers had assumed was the ship's seamstress, were "the quintescence [sic] of comfort and convenience. We were so plentifully supplied with flowers, candy, books and other items that we had to maneuver to find room for ourselves. . . . The food was too good, and the service matched it. What more can one say?"[64] While Lida Broner faced hostile train conductors, separate entrances, and suspicious fellow passengers, the Holtons found "our arrival . . . made most agreeable by the presence of no less than three representatives of the various travel bureaus."[65] The narrative focused on architecture, historic sites, the "indifferent food and service, always slow and usually grudgingly performed," and the hotel amenities.[66] Unlike Lida Broner's diary, the volumes contain few references to people, with most references to servants named by role, not name.

Also, unlike Lida Broner's photos, which look more like family snapshots, the Holton photos look strikingly like those in the Kodak ads focused on travel. The photo captioned "Leaving home" shows four fashionably dressed Holtons and two shiny late-model automobiles; following this, "Trix sees us off" features three women smiling at the train station, weighed down with accessories—gloves, hats, scarf, fur, suit-case, bag—pleased to be starting the journey. After a few shipboard pho-tos, the Holtons include shots of cathedrals, abbeys, monuments, ethnic "types" like "An Old Salt" and "Quaint Cottages," replicating the photo traditions encouraged by the Kodak ads. Two, titled "The Yeats's Daily Task" and "Yeats Sr. at Work," picture servants with cars, a theme ap-pearing in "Take a Kodak with you" ads. The Holtons' photo features two men packing bags on top of two shiny cars in front of an ivy-covered building. Short captions include value judgments such as "A Sporting Rolls," "A Fine Laburnum," and "Thirteenth Century Grandeur." Volume three includes a series of photos of a peace rally in Trafalgar Square with captions such as "Red Propaganda" (a poster), "Down with War!" (protest signs), "Another Crusader" (a woman passing out papers), and "Interested Spectators" (two fashionably dressed sporting women, obvi-ously amused, holding badminton and tennis racquets). The final shot in the Trafalgar Square series features seven bobbies, four of them look-ing at the camera, titled "Guardians of the Peace." Photos taken in Swe-den emphasize buildings, monuments, "street types," and a few shots of the travelers. Some document a visit to an open-air museum featuring dancers and a maypole.[67]

Both the Holtons and Lida Broner operated their cameras according to the suggestions made by Kodak. The Holtons treated England and Swe-den as a "Camera-Land," a series of places that existed for the amusement of the camera holder, while Lida Broner approached South Africa as a family reunion, a time to document renewed relationships. The Holtons' wealth and whiteness freed them from much discomfort and danger, but they also allowed these things to keep them aloof from the people of the places they visited. While they reported interaction with workers in the travel industry—guides, chauffeurs, hotel maids, innkeepers—they seemingly got to know few people, even as they moved among them. Racism put obstacles in front of Lida Broner during her travels, but as she engaged in activism and her trade while traveling, she immersed herself in the communities she visited: going to dances, participating in community events like weddings and funerals, and speaking at schools and churches. She used her camera as Kodak suggested for family life, not for documenting the storied architecture, monuments, and "foreign types" while on tour.

As the differences between the Holton and Bronner albums demon-strate, the connection between cameras and mobility did not so much extend from the white upper class (as depicted in advertising) as it emerged as a mass practice with different forms simultaneously informed by different levels of access to the public spaces of tourism. While the photographic marketing and much popular dialogue emphasized the touristic imperatives of the privileged, many others embraced both geographic mobility and portable cameras. Images of tourism in the public imagination emphasized leisure travel as a way to distinguish oneself as modern, technologically sophisticated, and cultured according to models provided by white cultural constructs, but often camera users employed the opportunity of portable photography to feature different identities from those pictured in marketing. They played with ideas about gender, race, sexuality, community, individuality, and mobility as they ushered in a new wave of mass cultural emphasis on the visual.

THE LEGACY OF THE FIRST
GENERATION OF MASS TOURISM
AND PORTABLE PHOTOGRAPHY

After dreaming of the possibility for almost twenty years, seventy-two-year-old George Eastman—inventor, industrialist, philanthropist, and recent retiree from Eastman Kodak—took a safari trip in 1926. Accompanied by two friends, banker Daniel E. Pomeroy and physician Audley D. Stewart, Eastman traveled to Kenya to visit Martin and Osa Johnson, celebrity travelers who specialized in documenting the peoples and wildlife of the African continent. Like other wealthy men of his time, Eastman had become fascinated by the safari hunt and longed to experience the excitement of pursuing some of the largest mammals on the planet. As one biographer noted, for Eastman, "the thrill of the kill on safari was augmented by the thrill of being in constant danger. It was enough to get his septuagenarian blood circulating."[1] The founder and former president of the biggest photographic company at the time was no typical hunter, however, for he traveled with at least six cameras, including the new Ciné-Kodak, a portable motion picture camera. Even the danger seemed secondary to the imperative to photograph it. Eastman funded a major film project led by the Johnsons to capture video and sound of African wildlife for the American Natural History Museum. He also killed "five lions, three rhinoceroses, and three buffaloes" to contribute to the museum's ongoing habitat re-creation project, while taking many souvenir photographs and videos.[2]

A year later, in 1927, Eastman self-published *Chronicles of an African Trip*, a photo-essay built on a literary trope: a safari taken by wealthy white travelers, one of many accounts of its kind published in the late nineteenth and early twentieth centuries. In 1907 Winston Churchill visited Africa, and in 1910 Theodore Roosevelt did the same. Both of them wrote about their travels as a way to justify white imperialism on the continent.[3] Eastman's *Chronicles* fell solidly in this tradition. The first two photographs in the document assert the image of the imperialist safari adventure but also the established wealth of the adventurers. The photograph captioned "Party at Lummuru, en route to Kedong Valley" shows Martin and Osa Johnson with Eastman, Pomeroy, and Stewart trainside, looking like explorers on the move in their jodhpurs, jackets, and safari hats. The text of *Chronicles* consists of letters written by East-man throughout the trip to family and acquaintances. In the first let-ter, Eastman recounts the trip to the port of embarkation in New York, with descriptions of dining and lavish attention and telegrams. This is accompanied by a photograph of the men dressed in suits, having tea with the captain of the ship. The image of the men in their clean suits taking tea from a silver service on crisp white linen reinforces the class position of the travelers.[4] Other photographs maintain the imperialist trope, such as a collage of four portraits titled "Headquarters at Nairo-bi," including named portraits of the white travelers and an unnamed Kenyan near the entrance to the visitors' quarters.[5] Other images of Ken-yans emphasize their roles as laborers or as white-imagined exotics. The camera was the key tool for establishing the social position of the trav-elers. Not only did it document the scenery, people, flora, and fauna of a place unfamiliar to the tourists and the audience for the album, but also its presence often directed the action itself.

Eastman frequently conflated the hunt and its documentation, but two photographic adventures stand out for the effect of the camera's presence on the action itself. On June 6, 1926, Eastman and his party encountered a rhinoceros. On determining that the rhino's "horns were not good specimens," recounts Eastman, "I thought I would try making a Ciné-Kodak of him." As he stood with his camera pointed at the rhino, the animal charged at him, and the photographer stepped out of the way at the last moment, just as his friends shot the animal. Eastman's account focuses not on the kill but on the filming of it: "I kept the camera trained on him all right but the film, we found on . . . developing it, appeared hopelessly over-exposed. . . . The affair could not have been more perfect if it had been staged and was the opportunity of a lifetime. I am much disappointed not to have got a good picture." Eastman's disappointment was short-lived, however; he provides a footnote assuring the reader that the film turned out all right when developed back at the Kodak labs in Rochester.[6] On August 5, Eastman wrote to Alice Whitney, describing an unsuccessful lion hunt in which the need to take photographs drove the actions of everyone and everything:

> On Monday, the 2nd, we had our forty spearmen out for lion for the first time. . . . We took them in three trucks to a donga [a dry ravine] where we had seen lions. . . . They advanced slowly, making little noise (contrary to my expectations), because they did not want to have the lion get out too far ahead of them. . . . Besides the three trucks we had the Buick, Osa's new Willys-Knight, Carl Akeley's two cars and Martin Johnson on his old Willys-Knight. . . . Half of the cars were on one side of the donga and half on the other with Martin in front with his camera. Akeley also had another of his cameras, and, of course, Audley and I had our Ciné-Kodaks and 1A's.[7]

Despite the forty hired hunters, seven vehicles, and six cameras, no one captured images of a lion that day. The hunt had become not an experience to document but a staged drama to capture on film. Near the end of his life, retired from the business of selling cameras and film, George Eastman had truly found a way to live out the promises made about photography in his company's advertising: the one in control of the camera would be the one who controlled not just the scene itself but the memory of it. In a more recent era, Eastman might have instructed the group to "do it for the vine!" His company, whose downfall is widely thought to have been the digital era, had certainly set the cultural model for documenting life in the digital age.

American leisure travel and photographic habits had fully interconnected by the middle of the twentieth century. While albums and scrapbooks continued to be popular, new technologies of mass recording, like improved flash cameras and moving-image cameras, allowed for differ-ent options. Projection-based sharing technologies like slideshows and film projectors—vastly improved over the previous century's lantern slides—allowed for vacation photos to become the home theater cliché of the postwar years. Such opportunities only cemented the cultural, social, and economic connection between mobility and personal ar-chiving, and the Eastman Kodak Company continued to lead in innova-tion in personal recording until the advent of the digital photography era. The vacation photos and albums produced with the first Kodaks now became less evidence of modernity than an antiquated set of ma-terials left from an earlier era, leading to archival decisions. While lo-cal archives grew in the Cold War era (especially around the time of the American Revolution Bicentennial and the book and film *Roots,* which touched off a new wave of interest in family and community history) to document the places in which the archives were located, the limited geographic mission of these bodies excluded the collection of materials that featured other places.[8] Some vacation photos currently in public ar-chives found their way there by donation, usually because the individ-uals represented were notable figures in the community. Other photos of more diverse subject matter, like those of Benjamin A. Haldane and Alice Austen, were saved thanks to the efforts of curators and scholars who recognized their value as evidence of the photographer's work. Be-cause of the racism that historically shaped collecting institutions in this era, photos and albums by people of color have been archived by families, not by institutions.[9]

The Kodak Company and its users together fused personal photog-raphy with mobility, but much of this connection formed according to the inequities of public space and the profit imperative of the corpora-tion. This dynamic set the stage for contemporary personal archiving habits on social media, particularly Facebook. Scholars of social media have shown that the centrality of the visual on Facebook imitates earli-er forms of memory making like the scrapbook and the yearbook, while others acknowledge the roots of social media visuality in family pho-tography.[10] Media scholars analyze issues of content ownership and the role of social media companies and advertisers in shaping individuals' constructions of memory on social media. Samuel Kinsley, writing in the journal *Cultural Geographies,* provides an important framework for understanding this dynamic. Building on Bernard Stiegler's concept of the "industrialisation of memory," Kinsley shows that "mnemotechnologies," the "technologies and technical supports that both support and reterritorialize what we collectively understand about our everyday lives," greatly influence our understanding of ourselves and our pasts.[11] Kinsley's position that the dynamics of mnemotechnologies need to be analyzed in the context of our conception of place is germane to tourist photography.[12] How did analog mnemotechnologies like the photo album, the Kodak, the Eastman Kodak business model, and, more broadly, systems of privilege and oppression in the age of the Kodak inform our contemporary uses of visual media for understanding of place? I hope that this work has shown that corporate facilitation of both social interaction and collective memory came with a price: Kodak marketing dominated public dialogue about personal photography and mobility, and the profit imperative naturalized the inequities in the access to public space. Some of the roots of Americans' contemporary touristic and photographic habits reach deep into the foundation of white privilege and class privilege in the United States. The Kodak Girl, a mobile young white woman embracing modernity, represents the role of white middle-class femininity in enacting that privilege.

Just as in the analog Kodak era, the digital era, however, offers possibilities for broader practices, as Web users have reclaimed the tourist photo as an important document of history and broadened access to primary sources that tell a fuller story of disenfranchised people reworking the dominant meanings of vernacular photography. In the Web era, online archives created by collectors, like Vintage Vacation Photos, a Web collection of scanned vacation slides produced between 1940 and 1970, as well as social media sites like Pinterest, Flikr, Instagram, Facebook, and Twitter, have allowed for the easy dissemination of photos and spurred new interest in vernacular photography. Projects like Trent Kelley's Flikr collection "Hidden in the Open," which documents African American male couples and same-sex affection in vintage photos—including vacation photos—became popular enough to warrant traditional media coverage.[13] Specialized vernacular photo interest groups have sizable followings, broadening support for the preservation of photos, and museum and historic site feeds rely heavily on photos, a fact made clear in early 2018 when snowstorms in the East and Midwest inspired #museumsnowballfight on Twitter, pitting institutions against one another for the most interesting snow-related images. Most important, as Amy Lonetree observes, historical visual material can provide inspiration and information needed by communities recovering from historical trauma. Of the profound effect of working with family photographs, she writes, "Locating my relatives in the archives has had great affective power in my life as they connect me directly to a rich heritage of resilience that I have the responsibility to simultaneously protect, produce, and nurture."[14] Such uses for photographs are possible only if photos are preserved, and for that they must be valued.

The renewed interest in and importance of historic photographs makes for new opportunities for public historians to help in preservation and dissemination. Historians can and should get involved in efforts to preserve and make available more of the record of vernacular photography, and particularly travel photos that get devalued. Oftentimes, travel photos fall outside the missions of local archives. Sometimes collectors—both private and professional—devalue travel snaps because of their reputation as ubiquitous and clichéd: "more vacation photos . . . [groan]." But as I hope this work has shown, much more can be learned from this body of material. Historians need to explore more fully the leisure practices of people of color, working-class people, LGBTQ individuals, and women, and their vacation snaps will provide key information. No tourist in history was a cliché; but historians' ideas about them have been. The historiography of travel has suffered greatly from Daniel Boorstin's classist separation of the traveler—the educated, upper-class, gentrified person capable of appreciating cultural exchange—from the tourist, the uneducated common boor wishing "everything to be done to him and for him." Boorstin located this change in the late nineteenth century and saw it continued into the time of his writing *The Image: or, What Happened to the American Dream* in the late fifties and early sixties. But when Boorstin noted that travelers in earlier eras had to experience hardship to travel but that present-day travelers experienced only comfort, he had never considered, for instance, Lida Broner or Adelheid Zeller or Pauli Murray.[15] Boorstin, and other intellectuals who followed his thinking, failed to account for differences among travelers, failed to consider the different power dynamics that shaped tourists' economic, political, cultural, and social access to spaces outside their own homes. Tourist snaps tell us a bigger, more complex story. Travel photos attest to mobility, limits, creativity, bigotry, values, experiences, relationships with others, power (or lack thereof), and humanity. Tourist photos should be valued as treasures because they are treasures, but much recovery work needs to be done so that the inequities informing their production in the first generation of portable mass photography may be confronted and denaturalized.

Many public historians—whether working in consulting firms, universities, archives, or museums—can find ways to identify, preserve, and make available more, and more diverse, collections of vernacular travel photos. History Harvests, a citizen history technique developed by William G. Thomas, Andrew Witmer, and Patrick Jones at the University of Nebraska–Lincoln, combines a community program with a digitization project. A historical organization sets a date, time, and place for the event, finds the necessary digitization equipment, trains volunteers or staff, and publicizes the event. It can be focused, like UNL's event on railroad history, or open, like UNC Chapel Hill's Community Histories Workshop History Harvest at Rocky Mills, North Carolina.[16] Smaller museums have also held history harvests. The Page-Walker Arts and History Center in Cary, North Carolina, collaborating with the Cary First Christian Church, held a history harvest focused on local African American history. Residents came to share their photos and documents, get them scanned, and learn from members of the African American Historical and Genealogical Society about researching their family histories.[17] Such events allow for exchanges of information as well as promote the preservation and dissemination of materials. A similar program is the Center for Home Movies' Home Movie Day. Started in 2012, the event occurs globally on the same day, at archives, museums, libraries, theaters, or universities. Each smaller event encourages people to bring their home movies to show and digitize. The sponsoring organization sets up the equipment and provides expertise on caring for, digitizing, and sharing home movies.[18] Historians play a key role in promoting historical themes through vernacular photography, such as in *Reflections in Black and White*, an exhibit curated by Janet Davidson at the Cape Fear Museum in Wilmington, North Carolina, that used black-and-white snapshots to encourage visitors to think about racial segregation. Davidson noted that "when you look at these images as a group, they give us a chance to reflect on how legally-sanctioned racial segregation helped shape people's daily lives. We want today's visitors to have a chance to imagine what it felt like to live in a world where Jim Crow laws and attitudes deeply affected the textures of daily life."[19] In addition to bringing direct historical expertise to the preservation and educational use of vernacular photographs, historians, who usually have wide professional and social media networks, can support historical organizations in their fund-raising efforts.

While historical organizations are rich resources for collecting and preserving vernacular photos, families and individual community members often take on this role. Some of the richest collections in archives and museums began as private collections in the hands of family members and descendants. Historians can help community and family collectors by advocating for the importance of diverse primary source types, assisting with digitization and preservation efforts, and using non-public archives as source materials for research. Collections managers and historians often pair to host family photo preservation events. The Association for Library Collections and Technical Services offers a free webinar called "The Preservation of Family Photographs: Here, There, and Everywhere" as well as a preservation advice column, "Ask Dear Donia."[20] Local libraries and museums regularly host family photo preservation events, sometimes in conjunction with genealogy programs. Cultural institutions are also addressing a significant need for guidance on personal archiving, addressing issues of privacy, organization, and digital legacy.[21]

The present effects of the first wave of portable mass photography go beyond the preservation of photographs, though; many of the inequities that informed mass tourism and the mass production of memory still exist. Between 1888 and the 1930s, transportation became more accessible and the tourism industry grew to offer more and better services, but many travelers faced major obstacles set in place by economic, racial, and other forms of inequality. This legacy, combined with the cultural association of travel with wealth, persists. Scholarship on travel and tourism documents well-founded fears around safety and economics that keep minorities and economically disadvantaged people from opportunities for travel. In summing up recent studies on tourism and economic equality, the leisure services scholar David Scott wrote that the "reality is that poorer Americans face formidable barriers and constraints to accessing public and private recreation amenities."[22] Culture has played a role in emphasizing that travel is for the privileged, as the images promoted by Kodak advertising in the early twentieth century have persisted as much as the exclusivity of the travel industry. The environmental science scholar Carolyn Finney asserts the relationship between culture and practice by noting that "racialization and representation are not passive processes. They also have the power to determine who actually participates in environmental activities and who does not."[23] Despite practical and cultural obstacles, however, individuals disadvantaged by racism, sexism, homophobia, and poverty managed to travel. Lida Broner, Adelheid Zeller, Pauli Murray, and others who left photos and diaries relating to their travels and the major impacts these experiences had on their lives show us that the barriers did not hold. These historical moments are instructive in helping us remove present obstacles. Potential travelers can take inspiration from these past examples, and contemporary scholars of leisure—including public historians—can mine these cases to understand the ways in which this first generation of tourist photographers cracked the barriers and told their stories. These travelers embraced the transformative power of travel by combining leisure with work, creatively planning transportation, standing up to inequities in services, sharing experiences through photos, and making spaces away from the surveillance of dominant cultures. Such strategies should not have then and should not today be the sole responsibility of tourists of color, poorer travelers, and sexual minorities, however. Public historians with privilege should use it to commit to removing obstacles and to creating inviting environments for all visitors to the spaces of history. Historians can and should continue to critically engage in analyzing travel practices that are socially, economically, politically, environmentally, and culturally deleterious. Irresponsible travel practices damage communities, cultural heritage, and the environment, and such practices need public historians' fuller analysis of their present outlines and their historical roots.

Historians' work positions them to deal effectively with breaking down the barriers to travel faced by minorities and/or economically disadvantaged people. By uncovering the diversity of travel practices, historians can debunk the dominant cultural association of travel with wealth that keeps many from following their dreams of motion. Similarly, archival projects to preserve and share the materials produced by past travel can benefit from the support of historians. Whether working in museums, consulting firms, universities, libraries, preservation agencies, or businesses, historians can look for ways to support and collaborate with organizations working to break down the obstacles in the way of travel or eliminate destructive tourism. Nonprofits like Outdoor Afro, which focuses on supporting African Americans' efforts to enjoy outdoor leisure and transform the environmental movement, and industry groups like the International Gay and Lesbian Travel Association, which provides resources for travel businesses and LGBT travelers, offer replicable models for facilitating travel as well as resources for identifying potential collaborators. Historians working in universities can craft student travel possibilities that respond to the needs of both underserved student travelers and visited communities. Historians working with communities can support efforts of groups like Sister Cities that facilitate exchange.

Finally, historians can help to preserve photo technologies and techniques, for while film can still be bought and used, person-to-person instruction and developing services can be hard to find. Film photography skills need to be preserved just as the photos themselves need saving. In the summer of 2017, after a few YouTube instructional videos and a perusal of the Kodak Brownie no. 2 user's manual, I opened my box camera (bought for seven dollars at an estate sale) to clean it and load it with film. My fear of damaging the camera in my ignorance made this process slow, and I carefully numbered and counted the tiny screws I removed from its face. Once cleaned, the camera needed loading. Thinking I'd certainly somehow expose all the film in fumbling about to load it, I took a painfully long time to consult the user's manual and drag the film from its spool to the other winding spool. Once it was secured, I turned the key, depriving myself of one of the eight possible exposures by mistaking the number 1 appearing in the tiny round window for a hash mark, but I was ready to take pictures. In an exciting five minutes, my roll was gone. Luckily, I had located a photography store nearby that processed 120 film, and by even greater luck met Emanuel and Ernest Cole of the Fotoshoppe in Cary, North Carolina, who took my first roll into the darkroom to remove from the Brownie. They developed the film and made a CD that held seven photos of varying quality (each having cost me—including film, the cost of the camera picked up at an estate sale, and developing—about nine dollars each!). Some were way too dark, even those taken outdoors. Some had their subjects partially in shade and partially in bright sun, which meant the image was washed out on one side and too dark on the other.

One turned out nicely: a portrait of the "Strolling Professor," a beloved statue on the campus of North Carolina State University of a professor reading while walking. Behind the professor, students sat with their phones, not caring about the person moving a black box around before them looking through the viewfinder. The light leak that would eventually become a problem in the camera was just starting when I snapped the "Strolling Professor" shot, and it softened the image toward the edges of the photo. Without the students and their phones and the parked cars in the background, it would have looked like a shot taken in the early years of the twentieth century, when the real "Strolling Professor," chemistry innovator William R. Johnston, was born in 1912, but way before the university dedicated his statue in 1986, at the beginning of the era of digital photography. My effort to use a Kodak Brownie helped me understand some of the exigencies faced by tourists around the turn of the twentieth century. I learned that one could not easily snap a good photo on a whim. Brownie photos required a careful assessment of the light, and, if people were the subject, their cooperation proved helpful as I took time to locate them in the tiny viewfinder. Having only eight exposures per roll led me to consider photo opportunities much more carefully than when taking digital photos. It also explained why, in contrast to today, I found so few photos of food in vacationers' albums: the light indoors was just never bright enough, and the interruption to the meal was significant. No wonder in 1901 Marian Peabody worried about being a "cheeky Kodak fiend." With such conditions for photography, I found myself trying to control the contents of the photo more intentionally. In trying to get a good photo of people, I got a little bossy. With the "Strolling Professor" shot, I enjoyed the result of my efforts, though, for in capturing a work of art and the people around it, the photo showed my fascination with the acts of both looking and moving. Such experiences helped me develop a bit more empathy for the ancestors using film, and without access to the legacy technologies and processes, I would lack understanding. Public historians of technology, like those at the George Eastman House who regularly teach workshops on old photo techniques, as well as photo experts like those at the Fotoshoppe help preserve the skills of the film age so that the intangible heritage of film photography may be preserved.[24]

This research emerged initially from a museum-related issue: the museum selfie. When I became interested in historical snapshots, the museum field was struggling with selfie practice, which was often named as an example of bad behavior on the part of visitors. In early 2016 the head of digital communications at the National Gallery of Denmark, Jonas Heide Smith, published a short essay on his blog *The Distant Sound of Trumpets*. The title was "We've Got 99 Problems but the Museum Selfie Ain't One." While flash photography does indeed damage objects, and visitors can be distracted by photos enough to inadvertently cause

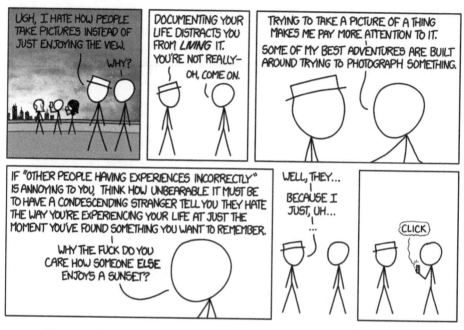

Figure 15. Cameras and "Other People Having Experiences Incorrectly," Xkcd: A Webcomic of Romance, Sarcasm, Math and Language, https://xkcd.com/1314/.

damage, most photography in museums is harmless. Smith acknowledged these problems but also emphasized that museums should not be over-policing their visitors and dictating the meanings they take from their encounters with art and artifacts. The cartoon he included at the end of the brief essay (figure 15) built on his final sentence: "So, let's by all means keep the discussions going, but here's to worrying mainly about, oh you know, real things in 2016."[25] While I would argue that people should always respect others and the contexts in which we find ourselves (especially if we are guests), and that sometimes photographic behavior can be as disrespectful as other bad behaviors, the act of taking a photo is not inherently disrespectful. Limits on photography in museums have been as much about enforcing "proper" (read genteel white) behavior as they have been about preservation. Contemporary ideas about snapshotting rely on ideas about public space—and who should really have access to it—formed in the Kodak era.

The roots of many museums' unease with visitor photography lie deep in the first generation of touring camerists, the era from 1888 to around 1930, when individuals took cameras about with them in their leisure pursuits, when some social strivers sought to prove they had been to the fashionable places and made themselves boorish in the effort, and economically and socially disenfranchised people started claiming public spaces with their lenses. While the marketing of cameras and film and much public dialogue centralized the ideas and values of status-conscious white heteronormative society (and even validated bad behavior), individual camera users of diverse backgrounds and different personalities used cameras and albums to create identities beyond the boundaries of prescription and proscription. Individuals took the opportunity of the photograph and of mobility to construct legacies for themselves that broadened the possibilities for freedom. When Kodak told consumers that their lives were connected to the nation's history, Americans took the company at its word. The strategy sold cameras better, perhaps, than the company had anticipated, but it also provided a new archive for historians to understand more fully the complexity and diversity of the past and thereby confront its legacies.

NOTES

Introduction: "The story is complete for all time"

1   I am using "they" as a singular pronoun because Murray was assigned fe-
    male at birth but strongly believed that they were male. While this is not
    a pronoun Murray used, it is an apt descriptor in our own time for an indi-
    vidual expressing gender fluidity, which Murray did. I also appreciate the
    approach of Murray biographer Rosalind Rosenberg, who addresses this is-
    sue before the introduction to *Jane Crow: The Life of Pauli Murray* (New York:
    Oxford University Press, 2017), xvii. "To use male pronouns for someone
    assigned female at birth in a time when that was not culturally possible,
    or gender neutral pronouns when, even to this day, no consensus exists on
    what those pronouns should be, I concluded, would undercut the immen-
    sity of the struggle in which Murray was engaged and the significance of
    her contributions."

2   Rik Smit, Ansgard Heinrich, and Marcel Broersma, "Activating the Past in
    the Ferguson Protests: Memory Work, Digital Activism and the Politics of
    Platforms," *New Media and Society* 20, no. 9 (2017): 3123. For other studies
    on the ways in which social media inform memory, see Katie Day Good,
    "From Scrapbook to Facebook: A History of Personal Media Assemblage and
    Archives," *New Media and Society* 15, no. 4 (2012): 557–73; Sergio Davalos et
    al., "'The Good Old Days: An Examination of Nostalgia in Facebook Posts,"
    International Journal of Human-Computer Studies 83 (2015): 83–93; Samuel
    Kinsley, "Memory Programmes: The Industrial Retention of Collective Life,"
    Cultural Geographies 22, no. 1 (2015): 155–75; Brian F. Clark, "From Yearbooks

to Facebook: Public Memory in Transition," *International Journal of the Book* 10 (2013): 19–25; Kathleen Richardson and Sue Hessey, "Archiving the Self? Facebook as Biography of Social and Relational Memory," *Journal of Information, Communication, and Ethics in Society* 7, no. 1 (2009): 25–38; Donell Holloway and Lelia Green, "Mediated Memory Making: The Virtual Family Photograph Album," *Communications* 42, no. 3 (2017): 351–68.

3   "Make Your Kodak Record Authentic—Autographic," ad cut 3362, General Advertising Copy, 1918–1923, 4 of 10, AB (advertising binders), 205.24, no. 1, 1890–1930, George Eastman Museum Archives, Legacy Collection, Rochester, NY.

4   The Emergence of Advertising in America Collection (hereafter EAA), Duke University Digital Collections, http://library.duke.edu/digitalcollections/eaa, K0413.

5   Thank you to David Ambaras for this insight on the brevity of written information allowed by other novel technologies of the late nineteenth and early twentieth centuries.

6   "Let Kodak save the day," ad cut 5219, General Advertising Copy, 1923–1925, book 8, AB.

7   C. B. Larrabee, "The Big Idea behind the Selling," *Printer's Ink* (July 1922): 30, quoted in Susan Strasser, *Satisfaction Guaranteed: The Making of the American Mass Market* (New York: Pantheon Books, 1989), 102.

8   Carl L. Becker, "Everyman His Own Historian," *American Historical Review* 37, no. 2 (January 1932): 221–36, reproduced at American Historical Association, https://www.historians.org/about-aha-and-membership/aha-history-and-archives/presidential-addresses/carl-l-becker (accessed March 28, 2016).

9   Shawn Michelle Smith, *American Archives: Gender, Race, and Class in Visual Culture* (Princeton: Princeton University Press, 1999), 92–94.

10 The Smithsonian American Art/National Portrait Gallery Library houses the "Pageant of America" collection of more than seven thousand photos considered for publication in the fifteen-volume set. The New York Public Library digitized the collection and made it available via New York Public Library Digital Collections at https://digitalcollections.nypl.org/collections/the-pageant-of-america-collection#/?tab=navigation. For an overview and relevant links, see Elizabeth Periale, "The Pageant of America," *Unbound*, Smithsonian Libraries blog, https://blog.library.si.edu/2010/05/the-pageant-of-america/#.WWtk7j_eP9K. The work of the German philosopher Walter Benjamin was deeply influential in this area as well. His volume *The Work of Art in the Age of Mechanical Reproduction* (1935) looks at the political implications for art through its replicability.

11 Alan Trachtenburg, *Reading American Photographs: Images as History, Matthew Brady to Walker Evans* (New York: Hill and Wang, 1989); Susan Sontag, *On Photography* (New York: Farrar, Straus and Giroux, 1977); Roland Barthes, *Camera Lucida: Reflections on Photography* (New York: Hill and Wang, 1981). See also Weston Bate, Euan McGillivray, and Matthew Nickson, *Private Lives, Public Heritage: Family Snapshots as History* (Melbourne: Hutchinson of Australia, 1986); and Marianne Hirsch, ed., *Family Frames:*

Photography, Narrative, and Postmemory (Cambridge: Harvard University Press, 1997).

12 Nancy Martha West, *Kodak and the Lens of Nostalgia* (Charlottesville: University of Virginia Press, 2000).

13 John P. Jacob, ed., *Kodak Girl: From the Martha Cooper Collection* (Göttingen: Steidl Publishers, 2011).

14 Smith, *American Archives*, 113–35.

15 This is a particularly rich area of scholarship. For explorations of this topic focused on the post–World War II period, see Erina Duganne, *The Self in Black and White: Race and Subjectivity in Postwar American Photography* (Hanover: Dartmouth College Press, 2010); Patricia Vettel-Becker, *Shooting from the Hip: Photography, Masculinity, and Postwar America* (Minneapolis: University of Minnesota Press, 2005); and Leigh Raiford, *Imprisoned in the Luminous Glare: Photography and the African American Freedom Struggle* (Chapel Hill: University of North Carolina Press, 2011). For studies of the earlier period of photographic history, see Deborah Willis, *Reflections in Black and White: A History of Black Photographers, 1840 to Present* (New York: Norton, 2000); and Maurice O. Wallace and Shawn Michelle Smith, eds., *Pictures and Progress: Early Photography and the Making of African American Identity* (Durham: Duke University Press, 2012).

16 Hulleah Tsinhnahjinnie, "When Is a Photograph Worth a Thousand Words?," in *Native Nations: Journeys in American Photography*, ed. Jane Alison (London: Barbican Art Gallery, 1998); *Our People, Our Land, Our Images: International Indigenous Photographers*, ed. Hulleah J. Tsinhnahjinnie and Veronica Passalacqua (Davis: C. N. Gorman Museum at the University of California, Davis, 2006); Amy Lonetree, "A Heritage of Resilience: Ho-Chunk Family Photographs in the Visual Archive," *The Public Historian* 41 no. 1 (February 2019): 34–50; Tom Jones, Michael Schmudlach, Matthew Daniel Mason, Amy Lonetree, and James A. Greendeer, *People of the Big Voice : Photographs of Ho-Chunk Families by Charles Van Schaick, 1879–1942*, (Madison, WI: Wisconsin Historical Society Press, 2011; Mique'l Icesis Askren, "From Negative to Positive: B. A. Haldane, Nineteenth-Century Tsimshian Photographer" (master's thesis, University of British Columbia, 2006).

17 Malcolm Andrews, *The Search for the Picturesque: Landscape Aesthetics and Tourism in Britain, 1760–1800* (Stanford: Stanford University Press, 1989). See also John Taylor, *A Dream of England: Landscape, Photography, and the Tourist's Imagination* (Manchester: Manchester University Press, 1994).

18 See Julie K. Brown, *Contesting Images: Photography and the World's Columbian Exposition* (Tucson: University of Arizona Press, 1994).

19 On imperial relations, see Dennis Merrill, *Negotiating Paradise: U.S. Tourism and Empire in Twentieth-Century Latin America* (Chapel Hill: University of North Carolina Press, 2009); Rosalie Schwartz, *Pleasure Island: Tourism and Temptation in Cuba* (Lincoln: University of Nebraska Press, 1997); Christine Skwiot, *The Purposes of Paradise: U.S. Tourism and Empire in Cuba and Hawai'i* (Philadelphia: University of Pennsylvania Press, 2010); Frank Taylor, *To Hell with Paradise: A History of the Jamaican Tourist Industry* (Pittsburgh: University of Pittsburgh Press, 1993). On tourism and nationalism,

see Marguerite Schaffer, *See America First: Tourism and National Identity, 1880–1940* (Washington, DC: Smithsonian Books, 2001); Shelley Baranowski, *Strength through Joy: Consumerism and Mass Tourism in the Third Reich* (Cambridge: Cambridge University Press, 2004); Christopher Endy, *Cold War Holidays: American Tourism in France* (Chapel Hill: University of North Carolina Press, 2004); Anne E. Gorsuch and Diane P. Koenker, eds., *Turizm: The Russian and East European Tourist under Capitalism and Socialism* (Ithaca: Cornell University Press, 2006). On tourism and cultural capital, see James Buzard, *The Beaten Track: European Tourism, Literature, and the Ways to "Culture," 1800–1918* (Oxford: Clarendon Press, 1993); Richard H. Gassan, *The Birth of American Tourism: New York, the Hudson Valley, and American Culture, 1790–1830* (Amherst: University of Massachusetts Press, 2008).

20 Elizabeth Edwards, *The Camera as Historian: Amateur Photographers and Historical Imagination, 1885–1918* (Durham: Duke University Press, 2012).

21 Maurice Halbwachs, *On Collective Memory*, trans. Lewis A. Coser (Chicago: University of Chicago Press, 1992).

22 Jan Assmann and John Czaplicka, "Collective Memory and Cultural Identity," *New German Critique* 65 (Spring–Summer 1995): 125–33. See also Kendall R. Phillips, ed., *Framing Public Memory* (Tuscaloosa: University of Alabama Press, 2004); and Glen McGillivray, ed., *Scrapbooks, Snapshots and Memorabilia: Hidden Archives of Performance* (Bern: International Academic Publishers, 2011).

23 Alison Landsberg, *Prosthetic Memory: The Transformation of American Remembrance in the Age of Mass Culture* (New York: Columbia University Press, 2004). For a discussion of popular culture's effects on memory in more recent cultural history, see Alison Landsberg, *Engaging the Past: Mass Culture and the Production of Historical Knowledge* (New York: Columbia University Press, 2015).

24 Barbie Zelizer, *Remembering to Forget: Holocaust Memory through the Camera's Eye* (Chicago: University of Chicago Press, 1998).

25 Ellen Gruber Garvey, *Writing with Scissors: American Scrapbooks from the Civil War to the Harlem Renaissance* (Oxford: Oxford University Press, 2013). See also Susan Tucker, Katherine Ott, and Patricia P. Buckler, eds., *The Scrapbook in American Life* (Philadelphia: Temple University Press, 2006); and Jessica Helfand, *Scrapbooks: An American History* (New Haven: Yale University Press, 2008).

26 John Urry, "Mobility and Proximity," *Sociology* 36, no. 2 (May 2002): 255–74.

Chapter One: "One did not 'take' a camera"

1 For information on the Grand Tour, see John Towner, *An Historical Geography of Recreation and Tourism in the Western World, 1540–1940* (Chichester: John Wiley and Sons, 1996), 96–138.

2 Edgar Peters Bowron and Peter Björn Kerber, *Pompeo Batoni: Prince of Painters in Eighteenth-Century Rome* (New Haven: Yale University Press, 2007), 79.

3   Bowron and Kerber, *Pompeo Batoni*, 40–41. The Batoni portrait, *James Caulfield, 4th Viscount Charlemont, Later 1st Earl of Charlemont (1728–1799)*, is at the Yale Center for British Art, Paul Mellon Collection, New Haven.

4   Bowron and Kerber, *Pompeo Batoni*, 62, 43.

5   Bowron and Kerber, *Pompeo Batoni*, 66–67.

6   Towner, *An Historical Geography*, 33.

7   Mark Twain, *The Innocents Abroad* (New York: Penguin Books, 2002), 225.

8   Thank you to Kat Charron for key observations that clarified my thinking on Mark Twain's work.

9   Cindy S. Aron, *Working at Play: A History of Vacations in the United States* (Oxford: Oxford University Press, 1999), 70.

10 See Aron, *Working at Play*, chaps. 4, 5, and 6.

11 For more on early and mid-nineteenth-century styles of tourism, see John F. Sears, *Sacred Places: American Tourist Attractions in the Nineteenth Century* (Amherst: University of Massachusetts Press, 1989).

12 Marguerite S. Schaffer, *See America First: Tourism and National Identity, 1880–1940* (Washington, DC: Smithsonian Institution Press, 2001); Richard Gassan, *The Birth of American Tourism: New York, the Hudson Valley, and American Culture, 1790–1830* (Amherst: University of Massachusetts Press, 2008).

13 See Steven Hoelscher, "The Photographic Construction of Tourist Space in Victorian America," *Geographical Review* 88, no. 4 (October 1998): 548–70.

14 A number of these professional albums of "views" sold to tourists can be examined at the George Eastman House International Library of Photography and Film in Rochester, NY (hereafter GEH), http://www.eastman house.org/; 73: 0204, "Nîmes et Ses Environs," and 73:0205: 1–12, "Athens," are good examples of this type of photographic souvenir.

15 Carl Ackerman, *George Eastman* (Boston: Houghton Mifflin, 1930), 13.

16 Ackerman, *George Eastman*, 23–25.

17 Ackerman, *George Eastman*, 24–25.

18 Douglas Collins, *The Story of Kodak* (New York: Harry N. Abrams, 1990), 50–57; Nancy Martha West, *Kodak and the Lens of Nostalgia* (Charlottesville: University of Virginia Press, 2000), 20–22.

19 West, *Kodak and the Lens of Nostalgia*, 74–75. See also Marc Olivier, "George Eastman's Modern Stone-Age Family: Snapshot Photography and the Brownie," *Technology and Culture* 48, no. 1 (January 2007): 1–19.

20 Kristin Hoganson, *Consumer's Imperium: The Global Production of American Domesticity, 1865–1920* (Chapel Hill: University of North Carolina Press, 2007).

21 Kathy Peiss, *Hope in a Jar: The Making of America's Beauty Culture* (Philadelphia: University of Pennsylvania Press, 1998).

22 Susan J. Matt, *Keeping Up with the Joneses: Envy in American Consumer Society, 1890–1930* (Philadelphia: University of Pennsylvania Press, 2003).

23 Charles F. McGovern, *Sold American: Consumption and Citizenship, 1890–1945* (Chapel Hill: University of North Carolina Press, 2006), 100.

24 See the chapters in Aron, *Working at Play*, on tourist infrastructure and extending vacations.

25 James Buzard, *The Beaten Track: European Tourism, Literature, and the Ways to Culture, 1800–1918* (Oxford: Clarendon Press, 1993).

Chapter Two: "The World is mine—I own a KODAK"

1 Eastman Kodak Company, "The World is mine," digitized print advertisement, 1912, Emergence of Advertising in America Collection (hereafter EAA), Duke Digital Collections, http://library.duke.edu/digitalcollections/eaa, K0469.
2 Nancy Martha West, *Kodak and the Lens of Nostalgia* (Charlottesville: University Press of Virginia, 2000), 25. West provides a solid overview of Kodak's early advertising campaign. See also Susan Strasser, *Satisfaction Guaranteed: The Making of the American Mass Market* (New York: Pantheon Books, 1989), 102–6.
3 Cindy S. Aron, *Working at Play: A History of Vacations in the United States* (Oxford: Oxford University Press, 1999), 183–205.
4 Brandon Dupont, Alka Gandhi, and Thomas Weiss, "The Long-Term Rise in Overseas Travel by Americans, 1820–2000," *Economic History Review* 65, no. 1 (2012): 146.
5 William W. Stowe, *Going Abroad: European Travel in Nineteenth-Century American Culture* (Princeton: Princeton University Press, 1994), 15.
6 Christopher Endy, "Travel and World Power: Americans in Europe, 1890–1917," *Diplomatic History* 22, no. 4 (Fall 1998): 565.
7 The *Kodak Trade Circular* served local dealers from 1899 to 1927, when *The Kodak Salesman* replaced most of its function as a source of sales education for dealers. Its first issue of the circular best explains this function. See "Salutatory," *Kodak Trade Circular*, 1899. All cited circulars are in the Kodak Trade Circulars Collection at the George Eastman Museum Legacy Collection, Rochester, NY.
8 "Salutatory."
9 *Kodak Trade Circular*, December 1899, 4.
10 "June Windows," *Kodak Trade Circular*, May 1902, 8.
11 *Kodak Trade Circular*, June 1908, 10, and July 1908, 8.
12 "The Show Window," *Kodak Trade Circular*, April 1911, 26–27.
13 "A Clever Window Display," *Kodak Trade Circular*, May 1911, 8–9.
14 "Kodak Window Display Competition," insert, *Kodak Trade Circular*, January 1909.
15 "Tripled His Business," *Kodak Trade Circular*, September 1900, 2.
16 Letter to "Dear Sir" from Eastman Kodak Company, April 28, 1903, Advertising Binders, Kodak Ads, 205.49, two of two (1893–1903), George Eastman Museum Archives, Rochester, NY.
17 "The Principles of Advertising," *Kodak Trade Circular*, November 1912, 13–14.
18 Bruce Bliven, "Teaching the Nation to Want to Kodak," *Printer's Ink*, February 7, 1918, 112.

19 George Eastman to William A. Fisher, October 1, 1888, George Eastman Correspondence, George Eastman Museum Archives, Legacy Collection, Rochester, NY.

20 "The Kodak Camera," ad clipping, Advertising Binders (hereafter AB), 205.24, no. 1, 1890–1930, George Eastman Museum Archives, Legacy Collection, Rochester, NY.

21 See in particular K0014, K0031, K0034, K0437, K0041, K0044, K0052, K0435, EAA.

22 West, *Kodak and the Lens of Nostalgia*, 155.

23 West, *Kodak and the Lens of Nostalgia*, 131–32; K0431, EAA.

24 Robert Rosenstone, "Learning from Those 'Imitative' Japanese: Another Side of the American Experience in the Mikado's Empire," *American Historical Review* 85 no. 3 (June 1980): 572–73.

25 K0083, EAA.

26 West, *Kodak and the Lens of Nostalgia*, 109–35; Rachel Snow "Tourism and American Identity: Kodak's Conspicuous Consumers Abroad," *Journal of American Culture* 31, no. 1 (March 2008): 7–19.

27 K0074, EAA.

28 K0088, EAA.

29 K0100, EAA.

30 K0079, EAA.

31 K0174, EAA.

32 Alexis McCrossen, *Marking Modern Times: A History of Clocks, Watches, and Other Timekeepers in American Life* (Chicago: University of Chicago Press, 2013), 5. For a discussion of timekeeping in European history, see David S. Landes, *Revolution in Time: Clocks and the Making of the Modern World* (Cambridge: Belknap Press of Harvard University Press, 1983). For an illuminating study of the camera as a response to modernity in a British context, see Elizabeth Edwards, *The Camera as Historian: Amateur Photography and Historical Imagination, 1885–1918* (Durham: Duke University Press, 2012).

33 "What Rudyard Kipling Thinks of the Pocket Kodak," ad cut 537, 1896, AB.

34 K0468, EAA.

35 Adele O'Brian illustration in "The Only Way," *Kodak Trade Circular*, April 1913, 10.

36 K0053, EAA.

37 Finis Dunaway, "Hunting with the Camera: Nature Photography, Manliness, and Modern Memory, 1890–1930," *Journal of American Studies* 34, no. 2 (August 2000): 207–30.

38 K0165, EAA.

39 K0179, EAA.

40 Dunaway, "Hunting with the Camera," 228.

41 Kodak Company, "One-half the world," print advertisement, 1919, EAA.

1   William Ludlum Jr., "Side Trips in Camera-Land by Motor Boat," *Photo Era Magazine*, June 1915, 287.

2   "The Spectator," *The Outlook*, October 23, 1909, 369.

3   See Elizabeth Edwards, *The Camera as Historian: Amateur Photographers and Historical Imagination, 1885–1918* (Durham: Duke University Press, 2012).

4   Richard H. Gassan, *The Birth of American Tourism: New York, the Hudson Valley, and American Culture, 1790–1830* (Amherst: University of Massachusetts Press, 2008), 52–69. See also Steven Hoelscher, "The Photographic Construction of Tourist Space in Victorian America," *Geographical Review* 88, no. 4 (October 1998): 548–70; and Emily Greenwald, "On the History of Photography and Site/Sight Seeing at Yellowstone," *Environmental History* 12 (July 2007): 654–60.

5   78:1314:1–36, Montana and Wyoming, 1885, Medium Albums, George Eastman House International Library of Photography and Film in Rochester, NY (hereafter GEH).

6   80:0801:1–134, Snapshot Views of Mexico, 1903–4, Medium Albums, GEH.

7   Herbert B. Turner, "Odd French Corners for the Camerist," *Photo Era Magazine*, March 1920, 115, 116.

8   Godfrey Priester, "With a Camera in Italy," *Photo Era Magazine*, November 1927, 238, 243.

9   Thomas Carpenter, "Florida Impressions," *Photo Era Magazine*, December 1, 1921, 281.

10 Asa Milton Shurtleff, photograph no. A170–249vo-35, Arthur and Elizabeth Schlesinger Library on the History of Women in America, Radcliffe Institute for Advanced Study, Harvard University, via ARTstor.

11 Phil M. Riley, "Camera Rambles Near Home," *Photo Era Magazine*, September 1922, 133.

12 Frank Reeves, "Vacation-Photography," *Photo Era Magazine*, August 1928, 90.

13 W. Robert Moore, "Friendly Camera-Trails," *Photo Era Magazine*, April 1928, 200; unknown photographer, University of California San Diego Collections via ARTstor.

14 Louisa Stephens Wright, "Diary of Louisa Stephens Wright," in *Golden Adventure: A Diary of Long Ago* (Pasadena, CA: San Pasqual Books, 1941), 135, North American Women's Letters and Diaries: Colonial Times to 1950 (hereafter NAWLD), Rutgers University Libraries.

15 Maynard Owen Williams, "Adventures with a Camera in Many Lands," *National Geographic*, July 1921, 87, 90–91.

16 Williams, "Adventures with a Camera in Many Lands," 88.

17 Fannie de C. Miller, "Diary of Fannie de C. Miller," in *Snap Notes of an Eastern Trip from the Diary of Fannie De C. Miller* (San Francisco: S. Carson Co., 1892), 22, NAWLD.

18 Reeves, "Vacation-Photography," 93.

19 Williams, "Adventures with a Camera in Many Lands," 91.

20 "Editorial: American Camerists Touring Europe," *Photo Era Magazine*, April 1, 1925, 217.

21 Gertrude Levy, "The American Tourist and His Camera," *Photo Era Magazine*, May 1927, 249.

22 Moore, "Friendly Camera-Trails," 198.

23 "The Spectator," 370.

24 Katherine Fiske Berry to John C. Berry, April 10, 1919, NAWLD.

25 "Log of Private Car J'arilla, 1907," Eastman Museum Medium Albums Collection, 2008:0082:0001–53.

26 Rochester city directories, HeritageQuest Online.

27 Information on the Roths and the Kaelbers can be found in the Rochester city directories and the US Census collections of HeritageQuest Online.

28 "Log of Private Car J'arilla, 1907."

29 The album "Snapshot Views of Mexico, 1903–04" (80:0801: 1–134) in the Eastman Archives Medium Albums Collection at the Eastman House Archives, attributes the captions to "Mrs. Franklin," noting that her husband was Dr. Spencer Franklin. US Census records from 1900 list a Spencer Franklin, a thirty-three-year-old physician, living on West 80th Street in Manhattan with his wife, Grace (then twenty-four), son Richard (six), and mother, Mary E. Franklin, a widow of seventy. He is listed in the "Physicians" section of the 1903 New York City directory with a practice at 346 Broadway. Given the ages of the people depicted in the photos as well as the information about Spencer Franklin's occupation, it is likely that this is the family in the photos.

30 The Museo de las Momias de Guanajuato is still in operation. See http://www.momiasdeguanajuato.gob.mx/index.html.

31 Advertising cut 538, Advertising Binders, 1895–1907 (one of eight), GEH.

32 "With a Kodak in the Land of the Navajo," *Kodak Trade Circular*, February 1909, 4, GEH.

33 Carol J. Williams, *Framing the West: Race, Gender, and the Photographic Frontier in the Pacific Northwest* (Oxford: Oxford University Press, 2003), 146.

34 R. R. Whiting, "Indians on pike at World's Fair trying to prevent picture being made by reflecting sunlight from small mirrors into camera," Digital ID (digital file from original stereograph) stereo 1s03832, http://hdl.loc.gov/loc.pnp/stereo.1s03832; Library of Congress Prints and Photographs Division, and "Indians from the 'Wild West' at World's Fair," St. Louis, Digital ID (digital file from original stereograph) stereo 1s03833, http://hdl.loc.gov/loc.pnp/stereo.1s03833; Library of Congress Prints and Photographs Division, http://hdl.loc.gov/loc.pnp/pp.print.

35 Marian Lawrence Peabody, "Diary of Marian Lawrence Peabody, September 1901," in *To Be Young Was Very Heaven* (Boston: Houghton Mifflin, 1967), 202.

36 Williams, *Framing the West*, 142–46.

37 Martha Sandweiss, *Print the Legend: Photography and the American West* (New Haven: Yale University Press, 2002), 221.

38 Hulleah Tsinhnahjinnie, "When Is a Photograph Worth a Thousand Words?" in *Native Nations: Journeys in American Photography*, ed. Jane Alison (London: Barbican Art Gallery, 1998), 42.

39 Mique'l Icesis Askren, "From Negative to Positive: B. A. Haldane,

Nineteenth-Century Tsimshian Photographer" (master's thesis, University of British Columbia, 2006); Mique'l Icesis Askren, "Benjamin A. Haldane, Tsimshian (1874–1941)," in *Our People, Our Land, Our Images: International Indigenous Photographers,* ed. Hulleah J. Tsinhnahjinnie and Veronica Passalacqua (Davis: C. N. Gorman Museum at the University of California, Davis, 2006), 2–3.

40 Askren, "Benjamin A. Haldane," 2.

41 Askren, "From Negative to Positive," 14–23.

42 Veronica Passalacqua, "Richard Throssel," in Alison, *Native Nations,* 315.

43 "Young Indian man playing in a river," University of Wyoming American Heritage Center, Richard Throssel Papers, accession no. 02394, box 9, TP25, Throssel no. 112; "Crow man and woman inside tipi," University of Wyoming American Heritage Center, Richard Throssel Papers, accession no. 02394, box 31, TP473, Throssel no. 715.

44 Laura E. Smith, *Horace Poolaw: Photographer of American Indian Modernity* (Lincoln: University of Nebraska Press, 2016).

45 Amy Lonetree, "A Heritage of Resilience: Ho-Chunk Family Photographs in the Visual Archive," *The Public Historian* 41, no. 1 (February 2019): 36, 43.

46 See Hulleah Tshinhnahjinnie's story of losing photos in a family fire, "When Is a Photograph," 41; Veronica Passalacqua, "Find Sovereignty through Relocation: Considering Photographic Consumption," in *Visual Currencies: Reflections on Native Photography,* ed. Henrietta Lidchi and Hulleah J. Tshinhnahjinnie (Edinburgh: National Museums Scotland, 2009), 21–22; and Nicole Strathman, "Student Snapshots: An Alternative Approach to the Visual History of American Indian Boarding Schools," *Humanities* 4 (2015): 730.

47 For more on American Indian boarding schools, see David Wallace Adams, *Education for Extinction: American Indians and the Boarding School Experience, 1875–1928* (Lawrence: University Press of Kansas, 1995); Ward Churchill, *Kill the Indian, Save the Man: The Genocidal Impact of American Indian Residential Schools* (San Francisco: City Lights Books, 2004); and Clifford E. Trafzer, Jean A. Keller, and Lorene Sisquoc, *Boarding School Blues: Revisiting American Indian Educational Experiences* (Lincoln: University of Nebraska Press, 2006).

48 Strathman, "Student Snapshots," 734–40. Parker McKenzie's photos may be found in the Parker McKenzie Collection, Oklahoma Historical Society, Oklahoma City. Some digitized versions are available in the OHS online catalog, http://www.okhistory.org/research/manuscripts.

49 Tsinhnahjinnie, "When Is a Photograph," 53.

50 Jennie Ross Cobb's photos may be found at the Jennie Ross Cobb Collection, Oklahoma Historical Society, Oklahoma City. Some digitized versions are available in the OHS online catalog, http://www.okhistory.org/research/manuscripts. See also Joan Jensen, "Jennie Ross Cobb," in Tsinhnahjinnie and Passalacqua, *Our People,* 4–5.

51 Veronica Passalacqua, "Jennie Ross Cobb," in Alison, *Native Nations,* 314.

52 Laura Wexler, *Tender Violence: Domestic Visions in an Age of U.S. Imperialism* (Chapel Hill: University of North Carolina Press, 2000), 231–32.

53 Wexler, *Tender Violence*, 224, 240, 258, and, for the cricket club quote, the epigraph on 209, from Ann Novotny, *Alice's World: The Life and Photography of an American Original* (Old Greenwich, CT: Chatham Press, 1976). For the efforts of amateur photographers, see Edwards, *The Camera as Historian*.

54 50.015.3597, film negative, Alice Austen Collection (hereafter AAC), Staten Island Historical Society Archives.

55 50.015.3596, AAC.

56 50.015.4894, AAC.

57 50.015.3457, AAC.

58 50.015.3455, AAC.

59 50.015.3821, AAC.

60 50.015.3887, AAC.

61 For examples of ruins photography, see photos 3856–3860, taken at Pompeii in 1906, and photos of the Roman Colosseum, photo 3871 and others, AAC.

62 Alice Austen photograph, 50.015.3627, Collection of Historic Richmond Town, Staten Island.

63 50.015.3627, AAC.

64 50.015.3798, AAC.

65 For examples of photos from Tangier, see 50.015.4869, 50.015.4511, 50.015.4512, 50.015.3888, 50.015.3897, 50.015.4878, 50.015.4873, and 50.015.4503, ACC.

66 50.015.3595, AAC.

67 The Staten Island Historical Society Online Collections makes Austen's earlier photography widely available. Photos taken by Austen in the northeastern United States often depict interiors and social settings. As of December 2017, digital copies of the European travel photo negatives are available only on-site at the Staten Island Historical Society at Historic Richmond Town.

68 50.015.4255, AAC.

69 David Deitcher, *Dear Friends: American Photographs of Men Together, 1840–1918* (New York: Harry N. Abrams, 2001).

70 Deborah Willis's comprehensive study of African American photographers shows the diversity of their work, although she notes that the largest number worked in studio photography. See Deborah Willis, *Reflections in Black: A History of Black Photographers, 1840 to the Present* (New York: W. W. Norton and Company, 2000). For a more focused analysis of African American photography and the theme of freedom in the late nineteenth and early twentieth centuries, see Deborah Willis and Barbara Krauthamer, *Envisioning Emancipation: Black Americans and the End of Slavery* (Philadelphia: Temple University Press, 2013).

71 Willis, *Reflections in Black*, 3–15. See also the digital collection "J. P Ball, Photographer," Cincinnati Museum Center, http://library.cincymuseum.org/ball/jpball.htm.

72 Deborah Willis, ed., *J. P. Ball: Daguerrean and Studio Photographer* (New York: Garland Publishing, 1993), xvi; the booklet that accompanied the panorama is reproduced in this volume.

73 For discussions of photography and Black activists, see Maurice O. Wallace and Shawn Michelle Smith, eds., *Pictures and Progress: Early Photography and the Making of African American Identity* (Durham: Duke University Press, 2012); and Shawn Michelle Smith, *Photography on the Color Line: W. E. B. Du Bois, Race, and Visual Culture* (Durham: Duke University Press, 2004).

74 See in particular Jasmine Nichole Cobb, *Picture Freedom: Remaking Black Visuality in the Early Nineteenth Century* (New York: New York University Press, 2015).

75 On the history of marketing to African Americans, see Robert E. Weems, *Desegregating the Dollar: African American Consumerism in the Twentieth Century* (New York: New York University Press, 1998).

76 "Amateur Photography," *Cleveland Gazette*, July 10, 1886.

77 "'Comet' Camera," *The Freeman*, November 9, 1895.

78 For some examples, see "The Quaint Old Saboba," *Broad Ax* (Salt Lake City), November 14, 1896; "Trick Camera," *Western Christian Recorder* (Kansas City), August 12, 1899; "Geronimo Charges for Photographs," *Broad Ax*, June 1, 1901; "Portable Darkroom Cabinet: Something for Tourists Who Carry a Camera," *Cleveland Gazette*, June 22, 1918.

79 Willis and Krauthamer, *Envisioning Emancipation*, 129–208.

80 The Gladstone Collection of African American Photographs at the Library of Congress is an excellent resource for photographic documentation of African American military service between the Civil War and World War I; see https://www.loc.gov/collections/gladstone-african-american-photographs/.

81 Edward P. Jones, "A Sunday Portrait," in *Picturing Us: African American Identity in Photography,* ed. Deborah Willis (New York: New Press, 1994), 36.

82 "Young African American boy sitting on a case,", Gladstone Collection, Library of Congress, https://lccn.loc.gov/2010647702. The photographer is identified with "photographed by Black."

83 Cindy S. Aron, *Working at Play: A History of Vacations in the United States* (Oxford: Oxford University Press, 1999), 49.

84 Aron, *Working at Play*, 49–50.

85 Mark S. Foster, "In the Face of 'Jim Crow': Prosperous Blacks and Vacations, Travel and Outdoor Leisure, 1890–1945," *Journal of Negro History* 84, no. 2 (Spring 1999): 130. For more on African American mobility before the age of the automobile, see Farah J. Griffin and Cheryl J. Fisk, *A Stranger in the Village: Two Centuries of African-American Travel Writing* (Boston: Beacon Press, 1998); and Alasdair Pettinger, *Always Everywhere: Travels of the Black Atlantic* (London: Cassell, 1998).

86 Blair L. M. Kelley, *Right to Ride: Streetcar Boycotts and African American Citizenship in the Era of "Plessy v. Ferguson"* (Chapel Hill: University of North Carolina Press, 2010).

87 For a fuller analysis of African American protest against the segregation of leisure space, see Victoria W. Wolcott, *Race, Riots, and Roller Coasters: The Struggle over Segregated Recreation in America* (Philadelphia: University of Pennsylvania Press, 2012). For a discussion of consumerism as a central

feature of citizenship in the twentieth century, see Lizabeth Cohen, *A Consumer's Republic: The Politics of Mass Consumption in Postwar America* (New York: Vintage Books, 2003).

88 Foster, "In the Face of 'Jim Crow,'" 131–35.

89 William Pickens, *Bursting Bonds* (Boston: Jordan and Moore Press, 1923), 163–64.

Chapter Four: *"When I Send You a Picture of Berlin"*

1 K0259, Emergence of Advertising in America Collection, Duke Digital Collections, http://library.duke.edu/digitalcollections/eaa/ (hereafter EAA).

2 K0256, EAA.

3 Frank Fay, Ben Ryan, and Dave Dreyer, "When I Send You a Picture of Berlin (You'll Know It's Over 'Over There,' I'm Coming Home)" (New York: Harry Von Tilzer, 1918), sheet music, Library of Congress, https://lccn.loc.gov/2013562963.

4 *Discography of American Historical Recordings*, s.v. "Victor matrix B-21939. When I send you a picture of Berlin (You'll know it's over 'over there,' I'm coming home) / Arthur Fields; Peerless Quartet," http://adp.library.ucsb.edu/index.php/matrix/detail/700007061/B-21939When_I_send_you_a_picture_of_Berlin_Youll_know_its_over_over_there_Im_coming_home (accessed September 29, 2017). Earworm warning!

5 Ellen Gruber Garvey, *Writing with Scissors: American Scrapbooks from the Civil War to the Harlem Renaissance* (Oxford: Oxford University Press, 2013), 87–130.

6 Jay Winter, "Picturing War," in *The Cambridge History of the the First World War*, vol. 1, *Global War* (Cambridge: Cambridge University Press, 2014), 643.

7 Inge Hennemen, "Souvenir," in *Shooting Range: Photography and the Great War*, ed. Inge Hennemen (Antwerp: FotoMuseum, 2014), 143.

8 Dean T. Tarvin photograph, Vespasian Warner Public Library, Illinois Digital Archives, http://www.idaillinois.org/cdm/ref/collection/p16614coll15/id/119; Carl R. Smith photograph, Vespasian Warner Public Library, Illinois Digital Archives, http://www.idaillinois.org/cdm/ref/collection/p16614coll15/id/112.

9 Charles Gibson photograph, Vespasian Warner Public Library, Illinois Digital Archives, http://www.idaillinois.org/cdm/ref/collection/p16614coll15/id/22.

10 Ernest B. Ricks photograph, Vespasian Warner Public Library, Illinois Digital Archives, http://www.idaillinois.org/cdm/ref/collection/p16614coll15/id/100.

11 Clarence H. Dickey service record, Vespasian Warner Public Library Illinois Digital Archives, http://www.idaillinois.org/cdm/ref/collection/p16614coll15/id/205, and photograph, http://www.idaillinois.org/cdm/ref/collection/p16614coll15/id/16.

12 For more on the YMCA's role in World War I, see Christopher Capozzola, *Uncle Sam Wants You: World War I and the Making of the Modern American*

Citizen (Oxford: Oxford University Press, 2008), 92–93; Alan Dawley, *Changing the World: American Progressives in War and Revolution* (Princeton: Princeton University Press, 2003), 144–55; Nina Mjagkij, *Loyalty in the Time of Trial: The African American Experience during World War I* (Lanham, MD: Rowman and Littlefield, 2011), 118–20; Chad L. Williams, *Torchbearers of Democracy: African American Soldiers in the World War I Era* (Chapel Hill: University of North Carolina Press, 2010), 92–103.

13 Arthur Lloyd Fletcher, *History of the 113th Field Artillery, 30th Division* (Raleigh, NC: History Committee of the 113th F.A., 1920), 30, electronic edition, Documenting the American South, University of North Carolina Chapel Hill Libraries, http://docsouth.unc.edu/wwi/fletcher/fletcher.html.

14 Fletcher, *History of the 113th*, 66.

15 Ann Thomas, *The Great War: The Persuasive Power of Photography* (Quebec: National Museum of Canada, 2014), 30.

16 Fletcher, *History of the 113th*, 110, 69, 70, 72, 74; Janina Struk, *Private Pictures: Soldiers' Inside View of War* (London: I.B. Tauris, 2011).

17 K0297, EAA.

18 K0258, EAA.

19 W. Frank Persons quoted in "Must Have Home Letters," *New York Times*, June 10, 1918.

20 K0279, EAA.

21 K0303, EAA.

22 K0303, EAA.

23 K0309, EAA.

24 K0257, EAA.

25 "Cameras for Soldiers," *Kodak Trade Circular*, October 1917, 7, Kodak Trade Circulars Collection, George Eastman Museum Legacy Collection, Rochester, NY.

26 Jane Carmichael, *First World War Photographers* (New York: Routledge, 1989), 11.

27 "If War Comes," *Kodak Trade Circular*, June 1914, 6.

28 "Business," *Kodak Trade Circular*, January 1915, 1.

29 "All Kinds of Business," *Kodak Trade Circular*, September 1917, 2.

30 "'Over the Top,'" *Kodak Trade Circular*, December 1917, 1.

31 K0334, EAA.

32 "Emma Dixin [*sic*]" entry in 1910 US census, accessed via HeritageQuest Online; Cornelia Carswell Serota, "A YMCA Canteen Worker in the 'Great War': The Diaries and Letters of Emma Young Dickson," 5–10, unpublished manuscript, Emma Young Dickson Papers, Kautz Family YMCA Archives, University of Minnesota Libraries (hereafter EYD), http://www.lib.umn.edu/ymca.

33 Diary entries, February–April 1918, box 1, folder 1; April 12–23, 1918, box 1, folder 2, EYD.

34 Cindy S. Aron, *Working at Play: A History of Vacations in the United States* (Oxford: Cambridge University Press, 1999), 127–55.

35 Diary entries, April 21–May 5, 1918, box 1, folder 3; May 5–21, 1918, box 1, folder 4; May 21–June 2, 1918, box 1, folder 5; June 3–7, 1918, box 1, folder 6; June 8–16, 1918, box 1, folder 7, EYD.

36 Diary entry, June 28–July 16, 1918, box 1, folder 10; Emma Dickson to William B. Dickson, June 29, 1918, EYD.

37 Diary entries, July 17–19, 1918, box 1, folder 12; June 28–July 16, 1918, box 1, folder 10, EYD.

38 Diary entry, July 21–26, 1918, box 1, folder 14, EYD.

39 Diary entry, July 17–19, 1918, box 1, folder 12, EYD.

40 Diary entries, August 2–4, 1918, box 1, folder 16; August 5–15, 1918, box 2, folder 1, EYD.

41 Diary entries, August 15–31, 1918, box 2, folder 2; August 31–September 4, 1918, box 2, folder 3; September 6–11, 1918, box 2, folder 4; September 12–19, 1918, box 2, folder 5; September 18–21, 1918, box 2, folder 6; September 22–29, 1918, box 2, folder 7; September 30–October 19, 1918, box 2, folder 8, EYD.

42 Diary entry, November 16–26, 1918, box 2, folder 11; Emma Dickson to "Dearest Mother," November 18, 1918, EYD.

43 Diary entries, January 19–31, 1919, box 3, folder 4, EYD.

44 Blue Star Mothers of America, "About the Service Flag," http://www.blue starmothers.org/service-flag (accessed August 29, 2016).

45 Photograph, "World War I Honor Day Parade 5," Richland County Digital History Room, http://content.mpl.org/cdm/ref/collection/rchr/id/1750.

46 Photograph, "Flower Pavilion at World War I Honor Day Parade 16," Richland County Digital History Room, http://content.mpl.org/cdm/ref/collec tion/rchr/id/1787.

47 Eastman Kodak Company, "Historical Record of Annual Earnings and Their Distribution," in *38th Annual Report* (1941), 18, Wayne P. Ellis Collection of Kodakiana, John Hartman Center for Sales, Advertising, and Marketing History, Duke University.

48 Advertising cut 2885, Kodak Advertisements, 1914–1918, bk. 5 (205.38), Kodak Trade Circulars Collection.

49 "For War Purposes Only," *Kodak Trade Circular,* October 1918, 1.

50 Struk, 26–38, 52–68.

Chapter Five: "A visible token"

1 Eastman Kodak Company, *28th Annual Report* (1930), 14–17. Annual reports are in the Wayne P. Ellis Collection of Kodakiana, John Hartman Center for Sales, Advertising, and Marketing History, Duke University.

2 Eastman Kodak Company, *26th Annual Report* (1928).

3 Eastman Kodak Company, *28th Annual Report* (1930), 16.

4 Eastman Kodak Company, *38th Annual Report* (1940), 18.

5 Gertrude Levy, "The American Tourist and His Camera," *Photo Era,* May 1927, 248–50.

6 W. X. Kinchloe, "Landscape Photography in Florida as a Summer Vacation," *Photo Era,* July 1922, 12. See also J. Ronson Hall, "A Photographer's Holiday in Britain," *Photo Era,* July 1923, 3.

7   James D. Basey, "The Photographic Outfit for the Traveler," *Photo Era*, July 1924, 9, 11.

8   W. Robert Moore, "Friendly Camera-Trails," *Photo Era*, April 1928, 193, 198.

9   Herbert B. Turner, "Odd French Corners for the Cameraist, *Photo Era*, March 1, 1920, 115, 121.

10 Basey, "The Photographic Outfit for the Traveler," 9–12.

11 Roland Gorbold, "Photography on Tour," *Photo Era*, August 1926, 59.

12 Levy, "The American Tourist and His Camera," 248.

13 John McFarlane, "Permettez! Camera Adventures in Europe," *Photo Era*, July 1930, 12–15.

14 Cindy S. Aron, *Working at Play: A History of Vacations in the United States* (Oxford: Cambridge University Press, 1999), 206–27. Philip Deloria documents the travels of American Indians in this period through involvement in athletics and through work in the entertainment industry. See Philip Deloria, *Indians in Unexpected Places* (Lawrence: University Press of Kansas, 2004).

15 Aron, *Working at Play*, 213–19; Andrew Kahrl, *The Land Was Ours: African American Beaches from Jim Crow to the Sunbelt South* (Cambridge: Harvard University Press, 2012), 24. See also Esther Newton, *Cherry Grove, Fire Island: Sixty Years in America's First Gay and Lesbian Town* (Boston: Beacon Press, 1993); and Julio Capó, "Sexual Connections: Queers and Competing Tourist Markets in Miami and the Caribbean, 1920–1940," *Radical History Review* 129 (October 2017): 9–33.

16 See Blair L. M. Kelley, *Right to Ride: Streetcar Boycotts and African American Citizenship in the Era of "Plessy v. Ferguson"* (Chapel Hill: University of North Carolina Press, 2010); and Catherine A. Barnes, *Journey from Jim Crow: The Desegregation of Southern Transit* (New York: Columbia University Press, 1983).

17 Cotton Seiler, *Republic of Drivers: A Cultural History of Automobility in America* (Chicago: University of Chicago Press, 2008), 36–42.

18 Kathleen Franz, "'The Open Road': Automobility and Racial Uplift in the Interwar Years," in *Technology and the African-American Experience*, ed. Daniel Miller (Cambridge: MIT Press, 2004):,134–35.

19 Mark S. Foster, "In the Face of 'Jim Crow': Prosperous Blacks and Vacations, Travel and Outdoor Leisure, 1890–1945," *Journal of Negro History* 84, no. 2 (Spring 1999): 141–43.

20 *The Negro Travelers' Green Book* (New York: Victor H. Green and Company, 1956), 33–34, 39, University of South Carolina Libraries Digital Collections, http://digital.tcl.sc.edu/cdm/ref/collection/greenbook/id/88.

21 On white uses of cameras to perpetuate racism, see Elvi Whittaker, "Photographing Race: The Discourse and Performance of Tourist Stereotypes," in *The Framed World: Tourism, Tourists and Photography*, ed. Mike Robinson and David Picard (Farnham, Surrey: Ashgate Press, 2009), 117–37.

22 Mary Woods album, Southern Historical Collection, Wilson Library, University of North Carolina, Chapel Hill; Cadaine Hairston album, Robert Langmuir African American Photograph Collection, Stuart A. Rose Manuscript, Archives, and Rare Book Library, Emory University (hereafter RLAAPC).

23 Victoria W. Wolcott, *Race, Riots, and Roller Coasters: The Struggle over Segregated Recreation in America* (Philadelphia: University of Pennsylvania Press, 2012), 23–24.

24 Kahrl, *The Land Was Ours*, 89–91 and 115–54.

25 Folder "'Chicago' (?), circa 1920," box 81, RLAAPC.

26 Randolph-Mahan family album, box 83, RLAAPC.

27 Mary Woods album.

28 Folder "Seattle," box 81, RLAAPC.

29 See in particular Elizabeth Edwards's work on record photography during this period. Americans had similar photographic impulses, although these were not as organized as the efforts put forth by English photographers. Elizabeth Edwards, *The Camera as Historian: Amateur Photographers and Historical Imagination, 1885–1918* (Durham: Duke University Press, 2012).

30 Information on the Zeller family may be found in the US Census and City Directory collections of HeritageQuest Online.

31 Adelheid Zeller, snapshot album, Europe, 1922, 73: 253: 1–378, Medium Albums Collection, Eastman Museum, Rochester.

32 Ilbert O. Lacy and Adelheid Z. Lacy, *Dusty Lockport Pages* (Lockport, NY: Niagara County Historical Society, 1952). In the introductory notes, the Lacys indicate that the publication was an outgrowth of their main focus: a history of the Erie Canal. The Buffalo History Museum Research Library has a typescript by Ilbert O. Lacy titled "Cable Tow Canal Boats," but Adelheid Lacy is not named as a co-author.

33 See Carroll Smith-Rosenberg, "The Female World of Love and Ritual: Relations between Women in Nineteenth-Century America," and Leila J. Rupp, "'Imagine My Surprise': Women's Relationships in Historical Perspective," in *Women and Health in America,* ed. Judith Walzer Leavitt (Madison: University of Wisconsin Press, 1984); Estelle Freedman, "'The Burning of Letters Continues': Elusive Identities and the Historical Construction of Sexuality," *Journal of Women's History* 9, no. 4 (Winter 1998): 181–200.

34 John D'Emilio and Estelle B. Freedman, *Intimate Matters: A History of Sexuality in America*, 3rd ed. (Chicago: University of Chicago Press, 2012), 222–35; George Chauncey, *Gay New York: Gender, Urban Culture, and the Making of the Gay Male World, 1890–1940* (New York: Basic Books, 1994), 99–101.

35 Aron, *Working at Play*, 69–100.

36 Estelle Freedman addresses this dynamic and its implications for historical research in "The Burning of Letters Continues," while Susan Ferentinos discusses the problem for public historians in *Interpreting LGBT History at Museums and Historic Sites* (Lanham, MD: Rowman and Littlefield, 2015).

37 Sharon R. Ullman, "'The Twentieth-Century Way': Female Impersonation and Sexual Practice in Turn-of-the-Century America," *Journal of the History of Sexuality* 5, no. 4 (1995): 576, 578, 583, 599.

38 For more on local restrictions on drag and gay life, see Chauncey, *Gay New York*, esp. chap. 12, "The Exclusion of Homosexuality from the Public Sphere in the 1930s," 330–54; for Weegee's photo, see 330. For more on Weegee, see Samantha Baskind, "Weegee's Jewishness," *History of Photography* 34, no.

1 (2010): 60–78. For a detailed description of crackdowns in Long Beach, California, see Ullman, "The Twentieth-Century Way."

39 Linda L. Revie, "'An Adamless Eden' in Ingonish: What Cape Breton's Archives Reveal," *Journal of Canadian Studies* 44, no. 2 (Spring 2010): 96, 113. Revie's work on Liscombe's archive is a particularly effective and sensitive approach to the ways in which sexuality affected the development of a personal archive.

40 Rosalind Rosenberg, *Jane Crow: The Life of Pauli Murray* (New York: Oxford University Press, 2017), 2. For my use of "they" and "their" as singular pronouns, see note 1 in the introduction.

41 Patricia Bell-Scott, *The Firebrand and the First Lady: Portrait of a Friendship; Pauli Murray, Eleanor Roosevelt, and the Struggle for Social Justice* (New York: Alfred A. Knopf, 2016), 11–13.

42 Pauli Murray Papers (hereafter PMP), Personal and Biographical, photograph album, ca.1919–1950, n.d. MC 412, 24vf, Schlesinger Library, Radcliffe Institute, Harvard University, seq. 44, http://nrs.harvard.edu/urn -3:RAD.SCHL:13398990?n=44. The "Vagabondia" scrapbook is in the Pauli Murray Papers but is not available online; see Rosenberg, *Jane Crow*, 39.

43 Bell-Scott, *The Firebrand and the First Lady*, 14.

44 "The 'Life and Times' of an American called Pauli Murray," PMP.

45 Rosenberg, *Jane Crow*, 55–60.

46 "The 'Life and Times' of an American called Pauli Murray," PMP.

47 On Murray's activism in these years, see Bell-Scott, *The Firebrand and the First Lady*, 21–60; and Rosenberg, *Jane Crow*, 45–55.

48 See Bell-Scott, *The Firebrand and the First Lady*, 61–66; Rosenberg, *Jane Crow*, 81–96.

49 The 'Life and Times' of an American called Pauli Murray, PMP, seq. 64, http://nrs.harvard.edu/urn-3:RAD.SCHL:13398990?n=64.

50 For a fuller analysis of this work, see Susan Winnett, *Writing Back: American Expatriates' Narratives of Return* (Baltimore: Johns Hopkins University Press, 2012), 203–33.

51 The Gertrude Stein and Alice B. Toklas Papers (hereafter GSABT) are housed in the Beinecke Rare Book and Manuscript Library at Yale University. Digital versions of some items may be found at http://beinecke.library.yale. edu/collections/highlights/gertrude-stein-and-alice-b-toklas-papers (accessed July 27, 2017). Individual images discussed in the text are cited by object ID numbers.

52 "Gertrude Stein in the Luxembourg Gardens," GSABT, Object ID 9998128.

53 "G.S. at Aix les Bains '25 (?)," GSABT, Object ID 2041647. This may have been a proof. Notes on the face of the photo say that the image has not been retouched and that it will be printed in sepia. Thank you to Christine Jamet Lamberton for help with translation.

54 Christa Clarke, "An African American in Pre-Apartheid South Africa: The Cultural Biography of a Collection," paper presented at the College Art Association Conference, Washington, DC, February 3–6, 2016. Clarke is the author of the forthcoming volume *The Activist Collector: Recovering the Story of Lida Clanton Broner, an African American Woman in Pre-Apartheid*

South Africa. On Max Yergan, see David Henry Anthony III, *Max Yergan: Race Man, Internationalist, Cold Warrior* (New York: New York University Press, 2006).

55 Catherine Higgs, *The Ghost of Equality: The Public Lives of D. D. T Jabavu of South Africa, 1885–1959* (Athens: Ohio University Press, 1997), 3.

56 Tiffany M. Gill, *Beauty Shop Politics: African American Women's Activism in the Beauty Industry* (Urbana: University of Illinois Press, 2010).

57 Clarke, "An African American in Pre-Apartheid South Africa."

58 Diary, box 1, ser. 1, Lida Broner Papers, Newark Museum Archives, Newark, NJ.

59 Clarke, "An African American in Pre-Apartheid South Africa."

60 Broner quoted in Clarke, "An African American in Pre-Apartheid South Africa."

61 Broner created two photo albums and one scrapbook. At the time I visited the Newark Museum archives, the photo albums had been removed from view because of their condition, but I was able to access digital copies. I am grateful to Dr. William Peniston and Dr. Christa Clarke of the Newark Museum for making these available to me.

62 Diary, January 6, 1939 entry, box 1, ser. 1, Lida Broner Papers, Newark Museum Archives.

63 Receipt pasted in vol. 1, Charles W. Holton Family Scrapbooks, 1936, Charles F. Cummings New Jersey Information Center, Newark Public Library (hereafter CWHFS).

64 Narrative, vol. 1, CWHFS.

65 Narrative, vol. 4, CWHFS.

66 Narrative, vol. 1, CWHFS.

67 Vols. 1, 2, and 3, CWHFS.

Conclusion: The Legacy of the First Generation of Mass Tourism and Portable Photography

1 Elizabeth Brayer, *George Eastman: A Biography* (Baltimore: Johns Hopkins University Press, 1996), 484, 486, 488.

2 "Rhinoceros Rushed Eastman in Africa," *New York Times*, October 12, 1926.

3 For a full analysis of these trips, see Roderick P. Neumann, "Churchill and Roosevelt in Africa: Performing and Writing Landscapes of Race, Empire, and Nation," *Annals of the Association of American Geographers* 103, no. 6 (2013): 1371–88.

4 George Eastman, *Chronicles of an African Trip* (Rochester, NY: Privately printed, 1927), 8, 13, e-book, Hathi Trust, http://hdl.handle.net/2027/mdp.39015070411056.

5 Eastman, *Chronicles,* 19. For more information on the racial dynamics of photography, see Elvi Whittaker, "Photographing Race: The Discourse and Performance of Tourist Stereotypes," in *The Framed World: Tourism, Tourists and Photography,* ed. Mike Robinson and David Picard (Farnham, Surrey: Ashgate Press, 2009), 117–37.

6   Eastman, *Chronicles*, 39.

7   Eastman, *Chronicles*, 65.

8   Tammy S. Gordon, *The Spirit of 1976: Commerce, Community, and the Politics of Commemoration* (Amherst: University of Massachusetts Press, 2013), 118.

9   Lila Teresa Church, "Documenting Local African American History," in *Interpreting African American History at Museums and Historic Sites*, ed. Max A. VanBalgooy (Lanham, MD: Rowman and Littlefield, 2014), 61–73.

10 On the scrapbook, see Katie Day Good, "From Scrapbook to Facebook: A History of Personal Media Assemblage and Archives," *New Media and Society* 15, no. 4 (2012): 557–73. On the yearbook, see Brian F. Clark, "From Yearbooks to Facebook: Public Memory in Transition," *International Journal of the Book* 10 (2013): 19–25. See also Tony Walter, "Communication Media and the Dead: From the Stone Age to Facebook," *Mortality* 20, no. 3 (2015): 215–32. On the roots of social media visibility, see in particular Donell Holloway and Lelia Green, "Mediated Memory Making: The Virtual Family Photograph Album," *Communications* 42, no. 3 (2017): 351–68.

11 Samuel Kinsley, "Memory Programmes: The Industrial Retention of Collective Life," *Cultural Geographies* 22, no. 1 (2015): 156. See also Bernard Stiegler, *Technics and Time*, vol. 2, *Disorientation*, trans. Stephen Barker (Stanford: Stanford University Press, 2009). Chapter 3 of Stiegler's book forwards the idea of the "industrialization of memory." Have fun with that prose, though.

12 Kinsley, "Memory Programmes," 167.

13 Vintage Vacation Photos, http://vintagevacationphotos.com/index.cfm; Trent Kelley, "Hidden in the Open: A Photographic Essay of Afro American Male Couples," Flikr album, https://www.flickr.com/photos/hidden-in-the-open/albums/72157636646867885.

14 Amy Lonetree, "A Heritage of Resilience: Ho-Chunk Family Photographs in the Visual Archive," *The Public Historian* 41, no. 1 (February 2019): 50.

15 Daniel J. Boorstin, "From Traveler to Tourist: The Lost Art of Travel," in *The Image: or, What Happened to the American Dream* (New York: Atheneum, 1962), 84–85.

16 On the University of Nebraska–Lincoln's history harvests, see "History Harvests: What Happens When Students Collect and Digitize the People's History?" *AHA Perspectives on History*, January 2013, https://www.historians.org/publications-and-directories/perspectives-on-history/january-2013/history-harvests; and the History Harvest website at http://historyharvest.unl.edu/. For more on the Community Histories Workshop, see https://communityhistories.org/.

17 Michael Papich, "African-American History Harvest Helps Residents Trace Their Roots," *Cary Citizen*, September 21, 2017.

18 "Home Movie Day," Center for Home Movies, http://www.centerforhomemovies.org/hmd/.

19 "Reflections in Black and White," Cape Fear Museum, https://www.capefearmuseum.com/exhibits/reflections-in-black-and-white/.

20 For "Dear Donia," see http://www.ala.org/alcts/preservationweek/advice/ask; to access the free webinar, visit http://www.ala.org/alcts/confevents/upcoming/webinar/pres/042313.

21 The Library of Congress offers some helpful information for getting started on personal digital archiving events and teaching opportunities. See "Personal Archiving: Preserving Your Digital Memories," http://digitalpreservation.gov/personalarchiving/index.html.

22 David Scott, "Economic Inequality, Poverty, and Park and Recreation Delivery," *Journal of Park and Recreation Administration* 31, no. 4 (Winter 2013): 3.

23 Carolyn Finney, *Black Faces, White Spaces: Reimagining the Relationship of African Americans to the Great Outdoors* (Chapel Hill: University of North Carolina Press, 2014), 4.

24 The Eastman Museum, "Photography Workshops," https://eastman.org/photography-workshops-1.

25 Jonas Heide Smith, "We've Got 99 Problems but the Museum Selfie Ain't One," *The Distant Sound of Trumpets*, blog post, January 1, 2016, http://jonassmith.dk/weblog/weve-got-99-problems-but-the-museum-selfie-aint-one/.

INDEX

Page numbers in *italics* refer to illustrative matter.

Ackerman, Carl, 20
activism, 65, 67–68, 106, 108, 111–12, 115
"Adventures with a Camera in Many
   Lands" (M. O. Williams), 44
advertising: "Before He Goes," 79; to Black
   consumers, lack of, 65; class privilege in, 25–26, *27*, 32, *33*, 91; "The Day
   That Will Never Come Again," 81–82;
   imperialistic messaging in, 36–38, 118;
   "Jerusalem Regained," 79; the Kodak
   Girl in, 2, 31, 53, 121; "Kodak Simplicity,"
   32, *33*; "The Kodak Story of the War,"
   71–72, *73*; "Let the children Kodak," 35;
   on mobility and travel photography,
   28–30; on modernity and individual experience, 36–37, 38, 129; "Take a Kodak
   with you," 52–53, 71, 95; on wartime
   photography, 4, 13, 37, 76, 78–82; white
   privilege in, 2–3, 5–6, 10–11, 13, 92–93;
   "The World is mine," 25–26, *27*, 36. *See
   also* Eastman Kodak Company; travel
   photography
aesthetics, 40
African American Historical and
   Genealogical Society, 123

African Americans: beach vacation
   photography of, 97–98; civil rights and
   segregation of, 6, 68, 96, 105; queer relationships in photography, 121; tourism
   nonprofit for, 125–26; travel by, 95–96,
   111–12; travel photography by, 65–69,
   99–101, 106–8, 112–13, 120. *See also*
   Great Migration; racism and civil rights
   of Black Americans
agency. *See* self-determination
albums. *See* presentation albums; souvenir photo albums
American Archives (S. M. Smith), 6, 7
American Historical Association, 4
American Indian communities. *See* Native
   Americans
American Natural History Museum, 118
American Southwest, 44–45
Andrews, Malcolm, 8
architecture and ruins, photography of,
   40, 41–42, 48–49, 58
Aron, Cindy, 19, 67, 103
Arthur Fields and the Peerless Quartet, 74
assimilation, forced, 6, 56. *See also* Native
   Americans

Assmann, Jan, 8
Association for Library Collections and Technical Services (ALCTS), 124
Atwater, Grace, 97
Augustus, Edward, 16
Austen, Alice, 57–63, 104–5, 120
autographic Kodak camera, 4, 81, 82, 88
automobiles: class and access to, 23; photographic poses with, 99; touring with, 43, 90, 95–97. *See also* mobility; rail travel; touring

Bagoe, Helen, 84, 85, 86, 88
Ball, J. P., 65
Ball's Splendid Mammoth Pictorial Tour of the United States (exhibition), 65
Barthes, Roland, 7
Basey, James, 93, 94
Batoni, Pompeo, 15–16, *17*
beach vacation photography, 63–64, 97–98. *See also* swimming; travel photography
beauty industry, 112
Becker, Carl L., 4–5
"Before He Goes" (advertisement), 79
Berry, Katherine Fiske, 46
Black Americans. *See* African Americans
boarding schools, 6, 56. *See also* Native Americans
Boorstin, Daniel, 122
box camera. *See* Brownie camera
Brady, Matthew, 80
Broersma, Marcel, 3
Broner, Lida, 111–13, 125, 149n61
Brooklyn Urban League, 113
Brown, George O., 65
Brownie camera, 2, 5, 22–23, 61, 126–27
Brownwell, Frank, 22
Bullet camera, 52
Bull's-Eye camera, 52

Cambridge History of World War I (Winter), 74
"Camera-Land," 39
Camera Lucida (Barthes), 7
cameras: autographic, 4, 81, 82, 88; Brownie, 2, 5, 22–23, 61, 126–27; Bullet, 52; Bull's-Eye, 52; Ciné-Kodak, 117–19; Comet, 65; Pocket, 36, 52, 80. *See also* developing technologies (photo); Eastman Kodak Company
Cameras and "Other People Having Experiences Incorrectly" (comic), *128*
Cape Fear Museum, 123
Carcassonne, France, 42

Carpenter, Thomas, 42
Cary First Christian Church, North Carolina, 123
Caulfield, James, 16
Center for Home Movies, 123
Champney, James Wells, 19–20, *21*
Charles F. Cummings New Jersey Information Center, 111
Chautauqua, 19
Cherokee Female Seminary, 57
children: Kodak advertising campaign on, 35; in photographs, 20, *21*, 31, 48, 57, 61, 113; swimming and discrimination of, 98–99
Chronicles of an African Trip (Eastman), 118
Churchill, Winston, 118
Ciné-Kodak camera, 117–19
cinema, 9
Clarke, Christa, 112, 113
classical portraiture, 12–13, 15–16, *17*
class privilege: in Kodak advertising, 25–26, *27*, 32, *33*, 91; recorded history and, 2–3, 5; transportation access and, 23; travel and, 95. *See also* white privilege
Clement, William A., 99
Cleveland Gazette, 65
Cobb, Jennie Ross, 57
Cole, Emanuel and Ernest, 126
Collier's Weekly, 34, 37
Comet camera, 65
compensation for photographic images, 52–54
consumerism, 22–23, 34, 103. *See also* tourist industry
Country Gentleman, 79
Country Life in America, 36
Cuba, 41
Cultural Geographies, 120
Czaplicka, John, 8

Dangeli, Mique'l Askren, 8, 54–55
darkrooms for tourists, 94. *See also* developing technologies (photo)
Davidson, Janet, 123
"Day That Will Never Come Again, The" (advertisement), 81–82
Dear Friends: American Photography and Male Affection, 1840–1918 (exhibition), 63–64
Deitcher, David, 64
Deloria, Philip, 146n14
developing technologies (photo), 20, 22, 28, 35, 94
Dickey, Clarence H., 77
Dickson, Emma Y., 82–88

Dickson, William B., 83
digitization projects, 123–24, 151n21
discrimination in tourist industry, 95–96.
    See also white privilege
Distant Sound of Trumpets, The (J. H.
    Smith), 127
domestic travel. See also tourist industry;
    travel photography; names of specific
    places
Douglass, Frederick, 65
Dreyer, Dave, 72
drowning, 98
Du Bois, W. E. B., 65, 69
Dunaway, Finis, 37
Dunbar, Paul Laurence, 65
Dupont, Brandon, 27

Eastman, George, 20, 92, 117–19
Eastman Kodak Company: company
    infrastructure of, 28–30, 91–92; estab-
    lishment of, 22; on mobility and power,
    25–26, 27, 120–21; motion picture
    industry and, 37–38; on personal as
    national history, 4, 26–27, 91; privileged
    history and advertising of, 2–3, 5–6,
    10–11, 13. See also advertising; cameras;
    travel photography
Edwards, Elizabeth, 8, 40
Egypt, 43–44, 48, 49
Eltinge, Julian, 104
empathy, historical, 9
Encott, Walter, 30
Endy, Christopher, 28
ethnographic photography, 8, 40, 44–45,
    57–58, 96
etiquette, photography, 45–46, 95, 127–28
eugenics movement, 7
Everybody's Autobiography (Stein), 110

Facebook, 3, 120, 121
family history through photography,
    81–82
Fay, Frank, 72
female relationships, 59–63, 105, 108–11.
    See also gay communities
Ferguson, Missouri, protests (2014), 3
Finney, Carolyn, 124
Fletcher, Arthur Lloyd, 77
Flikr, 121
Florida, 42
flu epidemic (1918–19), 74
foreign travel. See tourist industry; travel
    photography; names of specific places
Foster, Mark, 67, 68
FotoMuseum, 76

Fotoshoppe, 126, 127
France: Austen's photographs of, 58, 60,
    61, 62; Kodak facilities in, 92; record
    photography in, 41–42; Stein in, 110;
    wartime photography in, 77, 79, 82–85,
    87
Franklin, Grace, 41, 48–52, 63, 139n29
Franz, Kathleen, 96
Freeman, Daniel, 65
Freeman, The, 65

Gabriel, Ralph Henry, 7
Gandhi, Alka, 27
Garden, Mary, 83
Garvey, Ellen Gruber, 9
Gassan, Richard, 41
gay communities: photography by, 6;
    queer relationships and photography,
    59–64, 103, 104–5, 108–11, 121; sexual-
    ity mores and behaviors in, 103; travel
    association for, 125–26; travel by, 95;
    violence against, 12. See also sexuality
gaze, 10, 38, 89, 96, 101
gender representation in photography: by
    Austen, 57, 58, 104–5; by Eltinge, 104;
    by Liscombe, 105; masculinity and, 37;
    by Murray, 105–8; by Stein and Toklas,
    108–11; stereotypes of, 93–94. See also
    gay communities; self-determination;
    women
George Eastman House archives, 100–101,
    127
German American immigrants, 101–3,
    111
Germany, 47, 58, 82, 86–87
Gibson, Charles, 77
Gill, Tiffany M., 112
Goodridge brothers, 65
Gorbold, Roland, 94
Grand Tour tradition, 15–16, 17
Great Migration, 66–67, 92, 98. See also
    African Americans
Great War, The (A. Thomas), 78
Green, Victor, 96–97

Haida, 54
Hairston, Cadaine, 97, 98, 100
Halbwachs, Maurice, 8
Haldane, Benjamin A., 55, 120
Harlem Renaissance, 92, 106
Harper's Weekly, 19, 21
Hayden, Dorothy, 106
Heinrich, Ansgard, 3
Hennemen, Inge, 76
"Hidden in the Open" (T. Kelley), 121

historical empathy, 9
historic buildings, photography of, 40, 41–42, 48–49, 58
History of the 113th Field Artillery (Fletcher), 78
History Harvests, 123
Ho-Chunk, 55–56
Holmes, Peggie, 1, 107
Holocaust, 9
Holton family, 111, 113–15
How the Other Half Lives (Riis), 38
Hudson River School, 41
Hughes, Langston, 69
hunting and photography, 37, 39, 41, 44, 117–18

idleness and vacation, 19. *See also* touring
Image: or, What Happened to the American Dream, The (Boorstin), 122
imperialism, 36–38, 118
individual and collective memory, 8–9
industrialization of memory, as concept, 120–21
Innocents Abroad, The (Twain), 18
Instagram, 121
"instant artifact" process, 32
International Gay and Lesbian Travel Association, 125–26
Italy, 15, 41–42, 58

Jabavu, Davidson Don Tengu, 111–12, 113
Japan, 32–34, *33*, 46
J. C. Coblentz Drug Company, 30
"Jerusalem Regained" (advertisement), 79
Johnson, Martin and Osa, 117, 118
Johnston, William R., 126–27
Jones, Edward P., 66–67
Jones, Lewis B., 31
Jones, Patrick, 123

Kaelber, John George, 46–48
Kahrl, Andrew W., 98–99
Kelley, Blair L. M., 67
Kelley, Trent, 121
Kinchloe, W. X., 93
Kinsley, Samuel, 120–21
Kiowa, 55, 56
Kipling, Rudyard, 36
Knatchbull-Wyndham, Wyndham, 16, *17*
Kodak. *See* Eastman Kodak Company
Kodakery, as term, 3, 10
Kodak Girl, the, 2, 31, 53, 121. *See also* advertising

Kodak Girl: From the Martha Cooper Collection, 7
Kodak Salesman, The, 136n7
"Kodak Simplicity" (advertisement), 32, *33*
"Kodak Story of the War, The" (advertisement), 71–72, *73*
Kodak Trade Circular, 28, 29, 30, 31, 52, 80, 81, 136n7. *See also* Eastman Kodak Company

Ladies' Home Journal, 25, 32
Landsberg, Alison, 8–9
landscape photography, 40–42, 43, 46
Larrabee, C. B., 4
Leslie's Weekly, 32, 81
"Let me go back to France" (E. L. Whiting), 87
"Let the children Kodak" (advertisement), 35
Levy, Gertrude, 45, 93, 94
LGBTQ communities. *See* gay communities
Life magazine, 36
Liscombe, Ella, 105, 148n39
lithography, 12–13
Lonetree, Amy, 8, 55–56, 121–22
Louisiana Purchase Exposition (St. Louis, 1904), 53–54
Lourdes, France, 61
Ludlum, William, 39
Lumkwana, Queen, 113

Makah, 54
male relationships, 63–64, 104. *See also* gay communities
marketing. *See* advertising
Maryland, 98
masculinity and photography, 37. *See also* gender representation in photography
mass photography, 2–3, 36, 69, 94–96, 119–20. *See also* Eastman Kodak Company; souvenir photo albums; travel photography
mass production of memory, as concept, 2–3, 5–6, 9
mass travel. *See* tourist industry; travel photography
McCrossen, Alexis, 36
McFarlane, John, 95
McGovern, Charles F., 22
McKenzie, Parker, 56
memory studies, 8–9
Methodists, 98
Mexico, 41, 48–52

military photos. *See* wartime photography
Miller, Fannie, 44–45
Miller, R. S., 30
minstrelsy, 104
mnemotechnologies, 120–21
mobility, 25–30, 91, 95–96. *See also* travel
  narratives; travel photography; travel
  portraiture, classical
modernity and individual experience,
  36–37, 38, 129
Monson, Frederick, 52
Moore, W. Robert, 43, 45, 94
Morocco, 60–61, 62
motion in photography, 59–61, 62–63
motion picture industry and cameras,
  37–38, 117–18
Murray, Pauli, 1–2, 105–8, 125, 131n1
museum selfies, 127–28
#museumsnowballfight, 121

national and personal history, Kodak on,
  4, 26–27, 91
National Gallery of Denmark, 127
National Geographic, 44
Native Americans: at boarding schools, 6,
  56; Deloria's travel project on, 146n14;
  Kodak ad and, 52–53; Monson's book
  on, 52; resistance to photographing by,
  53–54; tourism photography of, 45, 52–
  53; travel by, 95; uses of photography
  by, 8, 54–57; white violence against, 6,
  12, 56
Negro: An Anthology (collection), 106
Negro Traveler's Green Book, The (Green),
  96–97
Newark Museum, 111, 113, 149n61
Newark Public Library, 111, 113
New Jersey, 97–98, *98*
New Mexico, 45
New York Public Library, 113
New York Times, 79
Niagara Falls, 19–20, *21*
Nineteenth Amendment of the U.S.
  Constitution, 34–35, 92
Norway, 45–46

On Photography (Sontag), 7
Outdoor Afro, 125
Outing Magazine, 32
Outlook, The, 39, 45

"Pageant of America, The" (series, Gabriel),
  7
Page-Walker Arts and History Center,
  123

paintings: classical portraiture, 12–13, 15–
  16, *17*; at Hudson River School, 41
Peabody, Marian, 54, 127
Penfield, Edward, 32
personal and national history, Kodak on,
  4, 26–27, 91
Persons, W. Frank, 79
Phoenix Indian Boarding School, 56–57
photo developing technologies, 20, 22, 28,
  35, 94
Photo Era Magazine, 39, 42, 45, 93
photographer's holiday, as marketing
  term, 93. *See also* travel photography
photographic sovereignty, 53–55. *See also*
  self-determination
photographic vacation, as marketing
  term, 93. *See also* travel photography
photography. *See* mass photography; travel photography
photography etiquette, 45–46, 95, 127–28.
  See also public space behaviors
photography studies, 7–10
Pickens, William, 68–69
"Picturing War" (Winter), 74–75
Pinterest, 121
Plessy, Homer, 68
Plessy v. Ferguson, 68
Pocket camera, 36, 52, 80
poetry, 86, 87, 105, 106
Pomeroy, Daniel E., 117, 118
Poolaw, Horace, 55
*Portrait of Sir Wyndham Knatchbull-
  Wyndham* (Batoni), 15–16, *17*
presentation albums, 41. *See also* souvenir
  photo albums
"Preservation of Family Photographs, The"
  (webinar, ALCTS), 124
preservation projects of historical
  photograph collections, 123–24, 126,
  151n21
Pride and Prejudice (Austen), 16
Priester, Godfrey, 42
primitiveness, 5, 37. *See also* gaze; imperialism
"Principles of Advertising, The" (*Kodak
  Trade Circular*), 31
Printer's Ink, 4, 31
print media, 9
Private Pictures (Struk), 89
"productive" tourism, 19, 32. *See also* tourist industry; travel photography
prosthetic memory, 8–9
public space behaviors, 102–3, 127–28. *See
  also* photography etiquette
Puerto Rico, 41

queer relationships and photography, 59–64, 103, 104, 108–11, 121. *See also* gay communities

racial privilege. *See* white privilege
racism and civil rights of Black Americans, 6, 67–68, 96, 105. *See also* African Americans
railroad infrastructure, 23
rail travel, 46–47, 67–68, 96. *See also* automobiles; mobility; tourist industry
Reading American Photographs (Trachtenberg), 7
record photography, 40, 41–42, 48–49, 58
Reeves, Frank, 43, 45
Reflections in Black and White (exhibit), 7–8, 123
Remington, Frederic, 37
Revie, Linda L., 105, 148n39
Ricks, Ernest B., 77
Riis, Jacob, 38
Riley, Phil, 42–43
Rochester Carting Company, 46
Rode, Lucien, 94
Roosevelt, Theodore, 118
Roots (book and film), 120
Rosenberg, Rosalind, 105
Roth, George F., 46–48
Ryan, Ben, 72

safari adventures, 117–18. *See also* hunting and photography
same-sex love and photography, 59–64, 103, 104, 108–11, 121. *See also* gay communities
Sandweiss, Martha, 54
Saturday Evening Post, 4, 32, 34–35, 37, 71, 80
scrapbooks. *See* souvenir photo albums
Search for the Picturesque, The (Andrews), 8
"Season at Niagara Falls, The" (Champney), 19–20, *21*
segregation, 67–68. *See also* racism and civil rights of Black Americans
self-definition and photography, 5–6, 10. *See also* gender representation in photography
self-determination, 53–57, 96–97, 101. *See also* gender representation in photography
selfies, 127–28
sexuality, 103, 148n39. *See also* gay communities
Shaffer, Marguerite S., 19

Shooting Range (exhibition), 76
Shurtleff, Asahel, 42
Sister Cities organizations, 126
Smit, Rik, 3
Smith, Carl R., 77
Smith, Jonas Heide, 127–28
Smith, Shawn Michelle, 6, 7
soldiers' photography. *See* wartime photography
"Song of the Highway, The" (Murray), 106
Sontag, Susan, 7
South Africa, 111–13
souvenir photo albums, 9–10; of African Americans, 99–101, 112–13; of Clement, 99; of Franklin, 48–52; by Holton family, 113–15; of Mexico travel, 41; of Murray, 1–2, 105–8; of Roth, 46–47; wartime, 82–88; of Wheeler, 48, *49*. *See also* presentation albums; travel narratives; travel photography
Staten Island Cricket Club, 58
steamship travel, 23, 27, 68. *See also* mobility; tourist industry
Stein, Gertrude, 108–11
Stewart, Audley D., 117, 118
Stiegler, Bernard, 120
Stowe, William W., 28
Strathman, Nicole, 56
"Strolling Professor" (statue), 126–127
Struk, Janina, 78, 89
surfing, 97
survivance, 56
swimming, 98–99. *See also* beach vacation photography

"Take a Kodak with you" (advertisement), 52–53, 71, 95
Tarvin, Dean T., 77
Tate, Gertrude, 57, 58–63
Terrell, Mary Church, 69
"They All Remembered the Kodak" (advertisement), 34
Thomas, Ann, 78
Thomas, William G., 123
"Three Thousand Miles on a Dime in Ten Day" (Murray), 106
Throssel, Richard, 55
Throssel Photocraft Company, 55
time and space, 36, 58
Toklas, Alice, 108–11
touring, 15–16, *17*, 39–47, 90, 95–97. *See also* automobiles; tourist industry; travel photography
touring clubs, 46–48

Tourist Gaze, The (Urry), 10
tourist industry: activist agencies for, 125–26; classical portraiture of, 12–13, 15–16, *17*; darkrooms for, 94; discrimination in, 95–96, 122; Kodak's advertising campaigns on, 28–35, 92–94; rise of mass travel, 18–22, 27–28, 92–96, 119; wartime photography and, 74, 77. *See also* advertising; consumerism; mass photography; travel photography
Trachtenberg, Alan, 7
transportation innovations, 23. *See also* rail travel; steamship travel
travel narratives, 18–19, 77–78. *See also* souvenir photo albums
travel photography, 1–3, 120–29; by African Americans, 65–69, 97–101, 106–8, 112–13; of domestic travel, 42–43; of Egypt, 43–44, 48, *49*; of European travel, 15–16, 41–42, 48, 58–61, 94–95, 102–3; place-based organization in, 9, 10; preservation of, 121–22; privilege and differences in, 11–12; of queer relationships, 59–64, 103, 104–5, 108–11; rise of nineteenth-century, 19–28; studies on, 8; by women, 39–40, 45–46, 59–63, 102–5, 108–11. *See also* advertising; mass photography; souvenir photo albums; touring; tourist industry
travel portraiture, classical, 12–13, 15–16, *17*
Tsimshian, 54–55
Tsinhnahjinnie, Hulleah, 8, 54, 57
Turner, Herbert, 42, 94
Twain, Mark, 18, 41
Twitter, 121

Ullman, Sharon R., 104
University of Nebraska–Lincoln, 123
Urry, John, 10

Van Schaick, Charles, 56
Vintage Vacation Photos, 121
Vizenor, Gerald, 56
voting rights, 34–35

wartime photography: by Emma Dickson, 82–88; Kodak advertising on, 4, 13, 37, 76, 78–82; local histories with, 78–79; photography and historical memory, 74–76; uniform photo, 76–77
Washington, Booker T., 69
Watson, James Sibley, Sr., 41
Weinberg, Jonathan, 58
Weiss, Thomas, 27

Wells-Barnett, Ida B., *64*, 65
West, Nancy Martha, 7, 32
"We've Got 99 Problems but the Museum Selfie Ain't One" (J. H. Smith), 127
Wexler, Laura, 57–58
Wheeler, W. S., 48, *49*
"When I Send You a Picture of Berlin" (song), 72–74, *75*
white privilege: in Kodak advertising, 25–26, *27*; in rail travel, 46–47, 67–68, 96; recorded history and, 2–3, 5–6, 10–11; Shawn Michelle Smith on, 7; of travelers, 68–69; in travel photographs, 50. *See also* discrimination in tourist industry
Whiting, E. Louise, 87
Whiting, Richard Ross, 53
Whitney, Alice, 119
William A. Clement Collection, 99
Williams, Carol J., 52, 54
Williams, Maynard Owen, 44
Willis, Deborah, 7–8, 65, 141n70
window displays on travel photography, 29–30
Winter, Jay, 74–75, 78
"With a Kodak in the Land of the Navajo" (Monson), 52
Witmer, Andrew, 123
Wolcott, Victoria, 98
women: as culture keepers, 12–13, 92; description of photography by, 39–40, 45–46; queer relationships and photography by, 59–64, 103, 104–5, 108–111; voting rights of, 34–35. *See also* gay communities; gender representation in photography
Woods, Mary, 97, 100
work, photography of, 100
Working at Play (Aron), 103–4
"World is mine, The" (advertisement), 25–26, *27*, 36
World Traveller, 31
World War I. *See* wartime photography
Wright, Louisa Stephens, 43–44
Writing with Scissors (Garvey), 9

Yale University Press, 7
Yergan, Max, 111
YMCA (Young Men's Christian Association), 77, 82, 83
Youth's Companion, 32, 35

Zelizer, Barbie, 9
Zeller, Adelheid, 101–2, 125
Zeller, Paul E., 101–2

TAMMY S. GORDON is professor of history and director of public history at North Carolina State University. She is the author of *Private History in Public: Exhibition and the Settings of Everyday Life* (2010) and *The Spirit of 1976: Commerce, Community, and the Politics of Commemoration* (2013) and articles on the connections between historical memory and the leisure economy. She has two kids, two dogs, and wanderlust.